WIN YOUR NEXT HOUR

WIN YOUR NEXT HOUR

HOW TO GET UNSTUCK AND TURN YOUR DREAMS INTO REALITY

BY DANNY LEHR

MANUSCRIPTS
PRESS

MANUSCRIPTS PRESS

WIN YOUR NEXT HOUR

How to Get Unstuck and Turn Your Dreams into Reality

ISBN   979-8-88926-192-6 *Paperback*

979-8-88926-193-3 *Hardcover*

979-8-88926-191-9 *eBook*

TABLE OF CONTENTS

INTRODUCTION

It was beyond miserable. Water gushed out of my shoelaces as I made the bunny ears. The necessary double-knots required to keep the wet boots secured over my wet socks worked as a press, wringing out even more water. And as uncomfortable as wet shoes over wet socks are, nothing prepares you for putting on damp, cold underwear at 4:30 a.m. in a tent. But there I was, on top of a mountain in Alaska, sporting dirty, wet Ralph Lauren boxer briefs.

The nearest community of Ketchikan receives an average of 175 inches of rain each year, and it felt like my clothing had absorbed 174 of them during the hike in. I was with my friend Jeff, an Alaskan resident and outdoors writer, on a four-day summer trip to the top of a remote mountain that required a boat to access. We had not seen a single human soul during those four days. Probably fewer than thirty people summit the trailless mountain each year, and the reason why was becoming clear.

As the rain continued its assault, fog decided to join the party. And because nothing draws a crowd like a crowd, cold ocean air started creeping up the side of the mountain to see what all the fuss was about. I found myself neck deep in one of the most demanding experiences of my life, and I hated it. My mind was reeling.

This is stupid. I'm never doing this again.

That kind of self-talk is the fast lane to feeling sorry for yourself, which would make the experience even worse and possibly endanger Jeff and me. It was clear I had to change my internal narrative.

I'm not afraid of a challenge. Throughout my life I've made a hobby of biting off more than I can chew, and then just chewing it anyway. I love being outside in the wilderness and the adventure of things most people will never see or experience. And most of all, I have become much more than a flippant acquaintance with physically demanding tasks.

As a six-year-old, chubby blond kid, my first backpacking trip was a thirty mile stretch of the John Muir Trail through Yosemite National Park. I remember going up switchbacks near ten thousand feet in elevation and wanting to stop. But we couldn't. We couldn't just camp in the middle of the trail. The only way out was to take some breaks and push through until we were over the pass. These kinds of physically and mentally challenging experiences kept coming my way, and I eventually developed my own strategy for dealing with them.

The first day of high school soccer conditioning, I wanted to quit more than ever before. And that was the first time I remember using my trick, which became a superpower. I lied to myself.

If I just get through today, I can quit tomorrow. Just finish today. Just win this next hour.

Spoiler: I didn't quit after that day. Or the next day, when I made the same empty promise to myself.

I didn't quit during my freshman year of high school when I started wrestling, a sport that required high levels of technique and even higher levels of suffering, and discovered the unfortunate reality of my athletic prowess. Suffering is what I'm best at. This became my reality as I excelled in wrestling and later Olympic-style weightlifting, which required me to train heavy squats nine sessions a week.

Over the last fifteen years, I've seen the power in winning your next hour. Through my experiences in business and athletics, I've met and become friends with founders of Fortune 500 companies, Olympians, and people who have found their version of success in many ways. I've experienced and witnessed what it takes to go from the sidelines to success.

Dreams, goals, aspirations: they are all overwhelming when you're thinking about the final product. If you've never had a million dollars, the idea of starting a company that grows to over ten million dollars seems like an impossible task. If you've never been able to keep off the fifteen pounds you lost on a crash diet, how can you possibly lose one hundred pounds? If you've never run two miles without walking, how can you run a marathon?

I'm going to provide you with the tools you need to win. The tips and tricks that equip you with the discipline you need to get unstuck. To change jobs, start a business, lose fifty pounds, move states, or take on the Appalachian trail. The intimidation of beginning a new challenge is replaced by self-doubt and procrastination when the going gets tough. So, how do you achieve on days when you lack motivation? Why will waiting until you're "good enough" only lead to failure? How can you structure your days and weeks so you have the time to begin? How friends and other people can play a critical role in your success? You'll learn a goal setting plan that takes you from "I don't know where to start" to clarity on "the things I didn't even know that I didn't know."

If you are happy and comfortable in your current life and have no further aspirations, this book is not for you. However, if you want to take your life to the next chapter, next level, or next step, then you need to commit to winning your next hour. This is for you if you ever get stuck—stuck with the boss you hate, in the neighborhood you don't feel safe in, or in the body that makes you cringe when you look in the mirror.

Life is too short for regrets. Stop waiting and wishing and calling it living.

That morning in Alaska in the rainy, cold, and foggy pre-dawn hours, I started again. *Just win the next hour. You can do this for one more hour, then maybe the rain will stop. Maybe the fog will lift. Maybe Jeff will slow the hell down.*

As the morning progressed, my body heat slowly warmed the inside of my cold rain gear. We had stopped a few times to glass for deer. The fog lifted and I could see hundreds of miles out into the beautiful inside passage, a maze of ocean and island mountains. It was the most beautiful thing I'd ever seen. I had won my last hour and was ready for the challenge of the next hour, and the next three days.

A few hours later the sun was out, and I was drying my socks off on a warm rock. And that's when my next hour of battling gnats began.

Most people see the finish line or finished product. They see the fully functioning business they're trying to grow, or the gap between their current skill level and the top level of competition. They think in order to succeed in business or athletics they have to know how to get to the finish line. But that's not true.

You need to start. You need to find one step that will lead to the next. You need to win your next hour.

CHAPTER 1

IDEKWTHTS

Do you recognize that acronym? You've said the phrase. You've said it before making a bold move like starting a business or beginning a weight loss transformation. You muttered the line when the IKEA box spilled dowels and particle board throughout your living room. You definitely said it when you sat down to write an essay in school and the first time you changed a diaper. Oh, and don't forget about that one time...

With my wife working the graveyard shift, that crying baby was my responsibility. Plan A was very clear, simple, and precise: ignore her and hope she solved her own problem. But as our sixteen-month-old daughter refused to quit crying cold turkey, I needed a new plan.

Stumbling through the house, I entered the nursery and immediately took three steps back. The smell hit me so hard I had to check the door to make sure nobody had replaced the bedroom with a porta-potty from the nearby construction site. Not a freshly serviced blue box, but a midsummer sun-warmed-at-the-asparagus-festival sweat lodge of a porta-potty. Alternating between confusion and repulsion, I had to go in.

Turning on the lights, I was greeted by a giggling child. The crying was replaced by a huge smile as we made eye contact. She was so proud to show me her art. A modern piece for sure, more Jackson Pollock than Van Gogh. The finger painting began on her crib and sheets. In search of a larger canvas, she moved on to the walls and eventually her own arms and face. Because she didn't have any paint in her room, she opted for a different medium: warm, fresh poop.

Struggling to process the job I had been assigned, my only thoughts were that same phrase from the aforementioned acronym: I Don't Even Know Where The Hell To Start.

The fog of deep sleep was ripped away as I searched for a clear path toward clean-up (or perhaps a substitute janitor), but it was no use. Nobody else was around to do the job, and I did not have a manual to read or a YouTube instructional video to watch. Someone had to clean up the crib, the baby, the baby's pajamas, the sheets, and the wall. Bathing my daughter, packing up the car, and burning the whole place to the ground felt like the best option. Calling my mom and begging her to come over and helped seemed like the second-best choice.

While processing the unfortunate impracticality of those actions, the only real option I had was to begin. I just had to start.

Digging through the sheets using only index fingers and thumbs, I excavated my daughter. I wiped and bathed her, overwhelmed with relief as she goes back to sleep in the pack-and-play. After reexamining the scene, I exhausted a freshly opened tub of Clorox wipes. And then another.

The sheets went in the laundry, and the pajamas in the outside trash. Within thirty minutes, the harrowing adventure was over, and I was finally in the shower, nearly breaking the knob as the water couldn't get hot enough to cleanse my hands, memory, and soul. Back in bed, chuckling as I drifted off for a few hours of sleep before my 4:45 a.m. alarm started the day, I'd won. I'd won the hour and tackled a project better suited for the Exxon Valdez clean-up crew.

This isn't about parenting, or poop, or acronyms. It's about being forced into action. Taking the first step. Starting something overwhelming. Sticking with something that has proven more difficult than anticipated.

Dreams, goals, and aspirations all seem overwhelming from behind the starting line. And they often get abandoned because the first step takes the most nerve—the most courage. Especially if you've started before, then quit. Your subconscious, and regular conscious, remembers...so you're afraid if you start because you might give up again when it gets hard.

Maybe you're a professional procrastinator or label yourself a perfectionist, but striving for perfection is really your form of perverse procrastination. Your excuse for not moving forward.

Start with This

Over the last decade I've started businesses, won international competitions, and become friends with people who have achieved at the highest level imaginable. Through those experiences I've seen patterns. These patterns will help you do the difficult part—the starting.

Taking those lessons, I've created a system you can follow to achieve your dreams. The system is a protocol for you to follow that will lead you to success. The three-step protocol is called WIN. The first step, the W, is for "words." Here are real examples that show you how powerful your words are.

For the last four years I've known I wanted to write a book. Figuring I had better learn how to write, I spent a few months reading nonfiction books by famous authors such as Stephen King, Ray Bradbury, and Maya Angelou. Using the tips I learned to write a weekly newsletter, I forced myself into consistent practice and got the benefit of feedback from readers.

But then, after about a year, I stopped. A temporary forced closure of my business coupled with uncertain economic times pulled me away from writing. The project got abandoned, and I was "too busy" and needed to get more sleep. Those were real issues I needed to deal with, but I still had twenty-four hours in the day that could have been better utilized. As it turns out, not starting was taking up a lot of my time.

When it came to actually starting the book, I didn't know where to begin. Should I find a publisher or self-publish? How would I do either of those things?

When will I have time? What is the topic I want to cover? Will I stay motivated when it gets hard? Do I know enough to be an expert in anything? Will this project be the definition of "opportunity cost"?

You don't *do* anything when you're busy thinking about failing. So I did something that forced the action: I scared the shit out of myself.

While on a business trip to Nashville, I decided it was time to *do* something. Wanting to make the most of the trip, on the flight there I pulled out my power list notebook (more on the power list in chapter 3). In the back, I wrote one task that would make this trip a success:

"Meet someone who can help me write a book and/or get more speaking gigs."

I had no idea who, where, what, or when. All I knew was what I felt, my biggest desire and gut instinct at that time. I had conviction.

Let's get clear on exactly what that meant to me: "conviction." It's the gut instinct, unequivocal knowledge, angel on your shoulder, devil on your shoulder that will twist any data point or purposefully-misrepresent-biblical-passages-to-justify belief. It's when you know. You know what you need to do with or without a full stack of evidence. Clairvoyance of your future. A certainty deep down so strong that you question everything else you thought you knew. When you have conviction, the "how" isn't important. You can always figure out the "how" if you know "what" you are after.

The idea of telling myself what I wanted to accomplish over the next five days seemed odd. I had this weird internal conflict. If I wrote this down and made it more than just a thought, that gives it power. And that was terrifying. But I knew what I wanted. My conviction in the result turned my dream into my goal. It turned the weight I was burdened to carry into gas in my tank. *It's* now a real thing. *It's* no longer just a thought.

This was the inflection point. The time when a tiny action made a massive impact. I knew what winning looked like.

I had no idea who, how, where, when, or what I would notice. But one thing was clear: over the next five days I would meet someone or have a conversation that would help me get more speaking gigs and/or write a book. I just had one problem; I found that even saying it out loud was a challenge.

Why would I write a book? Who cares what I have to say? Sure, I have a story, but everybody does. This step is what stops so many people from pursuing their dreams.

A series of questions were reeling through my head. The same questions that haunt anyone who begins a new pursuit: What will people think of me? What if I fail? Who am I? Do I have a good idea? Do I have something to offer? Will people think I'm ridiculous when I tell them what I'm doing?

On my third day at the conference, Angela, a colleague from my business owners group, staggered to the table next to me and heaved a box onto the table. Opening the cumbersome cube, she began pulling out dozens of copies of a book. Glancing over, I saw her name on the cover. She had recently released a book, which she was promoting through keynote speaking engagements. And just like that, I had found the sign my subconscious was looking for.

My first step was telling Angela I was going to write a book too. That led to a high-five, followed by her advice based on her experience writing her own book. Finally, she introduced me to a college professor who leads a course that helps first-time authors navigate the process.

By facing my fear and having the courage to vocalize my goal, I ended up with a direct path to success.

W Is for Win (and Words)

A few weeks later, on my way to work at the Caffeine and Kilos HQ, I realized I can't be alone. The vulnerability of telling people your audacious goal must be challenging for everyone. I called my old weightlifting teammate, 2020 Olympian and three-time Pan American Champion, Wes Kitts.

As audacious goals go, a gold medal in the Olympics is toward the top of the list right below colonizing Mars and knowing what your spouse is thinking. It involves years of training, sacrifices, travel to competitions, drug testing, nutritional requirements and monetary struggles. You expect those challenges.

Then there are the other things: barriers you didn't think about; emotional and psychological blockades like verbalizing your goal to friends, family, and followers. Wes experienced them all.

"The first time I remember being hesitant to say a goal out loud was a few years before the Olympics. I was training to break an American record. I realized pretty quickly that if I can't even tell people, how can I really believe it myself?" he said. Without enough conviction to tell people about your plans, you'll never put in the time, effort, and energy it takes to accomplish the goal.

Wes went on to explain, "The thing about going for something big is, you're risking failure. Not only did I have the goal, but I needed to actually put the weights on the bar and lift it in competition."

But it wasn't the actual lift in competition that was scary. Training thirteen sessions a week prepared him for the event. The heart-stopping part was putting himself out there and telling people he was training to qualify for the Olympics, or training to break an American record. To a humble athlete who doesn't like to talk about himself, it was like bragging. In his good ol' boy southern accent, Wes explained the innocent act of telling people his goal was akin to "standing butt-naked in front of the mirror, just wearing it out."

His confidence climbed as he started by telling his mom, then high school football coach, and eventually whomever asked. Contrary to his initial beliefs, nobody scoffed at him. Nobody told him it was impossible. To his surprise, nobody pointed and laughed. What he got instead was an uprising of support.

"Self-doubt can silence your intuition and steer you away from even finding out what you really, really want," said business coach and entrepreneur Mario Lanzarotti in his TED Talk, "Stop Doubting Yourself and Go After What You Really, Really Want." But it doesn't have to steer you away, he argued. Instead of being a hurdle, it could be your superpower.[1]

Accompanying your self-doubt is loneliness. You're lonely because you're afraid—afraid you'll fail and that people will see you as a failure, afraid you'll see yourself as a failure. Everyone else seems to have it together, but you don't. You're filled with doubt. But this is actually your opportunity to succeed! Yes, you may fail. But if you don't try, you have a zero-percent chance of success.

Mario continued with the solution. "When you have the courage to be vulnerable and reveal your doubts with people you trust, you build a greater sense of trust within yourself."

By sharing your dreams and self-doubt, you remove the power they have over you. The loneliness of your secret disappears. Fear and doubt will always be a part of the human experience, but it doesn't have to be hidden under fake confidence. Resisting and concealing doubt gives it power over you. When experiencing doubt, relabel it as excitement. That doubt is often misplaced nervous energy. The feeling before you step on stage at the school talent show or before the big soccer game that we call nerves is often mislabeled as doubt. When you recognize it, tell yourself you're just excited for the opportunity to succeed!

People often reach out to me, as a business owner, to discuss ideas and plans they have for opening their own business. Ten months ago, I got a DM from Erica, my favorite barista in town, asking if I would give her just ten minutes of my time to answer a few questions about a business she was starting. Erica was leaving her job to start her own coffee trailer. We kept in touch over the following months as she navigated the yellow tape of construction and the red tape of city, county, and state permits. Of course, the branding, marketing, and selling also needed to be formulated.

How did she start? She bought a trailer and told someone what she was up to. By reaching out to people who have started businesses before, she gained business advice and confidence in herself. I reached out to Erica to interview her, knowing as a new business owner her story of starting was fresh in her memory.

"I wish I would have asked for help sooner. Everyone was so helpful and excited to be a part of it," she said.

What she would have done differently is rely on her relationships more. People loved helping her, and they couldn't have helped if she never told them her plans. She hesitated to tell her most trusted friends, but as she did they poured out belief in her and did everything they could to help.

Her dad helped with the construction, her brother-in-law (an engineer) with the interior design that had to pass a litany of local regulations. The owner of the coffee shop she was quitting went out of her way to assist with bean sourcing and drink pricing structure. Friends that have started businesses gave her lists of things to watch out for and told her where she should be focusing.

And what about you? What is the thing you want to do but are hesitating to start?

Maybe you're waiting for clarity on the first step. Maybe it seems like such a big project, the idea of even starting is intimidating. Maybe you're bound by self-doubt. Maybe the story you're telling yourself centers around your lack of time, knowledge, or discipline. Or maybe you're just scared. So, where do you start?

Start by sharing your dream with someone. Today is a great day for that! You can start with a small step.

This is how you're going to win your next hour: tell your dream out loud to something alive. A houseplant, cat, or dog is the best place to start. Once you've said it out loud a few times, move to the mirror. Tell yourself what you're going to do. Look yourself in the eye, and say what you're going to accomplish. I usually like to end this with a wink, as if to say, Looking good there, self.

Failure Is an Option

But hold on. What if you fail? What if you tell people, and you don't accomplish what you say you're going to do?

During a packed concert, musician Macklemore started an on-stage dance off. The musician pulled in some fans from the crowd and gave them a shot to shake it. The first contestant was Willow.

She burst onto the scene, went for "her move," and the worst thing imaginable happened. Her planted left foot hit a wet spot, and she crashed into the stage like a WWE star bringing down the People's Elbow in front of thousands.

At the end of the competition, Macklemore grabbed the microphone and said, "The thing I love the most about this dance off is Willow. You know why? Because you showed us what we all do in life. I've slipped before. I've slipped in front of the entire world before. And you know what you did? You got back up and you kept dancing."[2]

The entire crowd began chanting. Not the name of the artist they each paid hundreds of dollars to watch perform, but the name of the girl who just slipped on stage. "Willow, Willow, Willow!"

You may fail. If you keep trying cool stuff, you definitely will. Who cares? Everybody fails. Everybody has made mistakes. But many people have never gone after their dreams. The only way to guarantee you don't succeed is to not try. Just by trying, you increase your chances of success.

Now send a text to someone who loves you and whom you trust. Just write, "Hey, I've been meaning to tell you, but I'm so nervous. I'm going to…"

Boom! In less than one hour, you've stepped off the cliff. Your confidant will ask some follow up questions, and now your dream has turned into a goal you're pursuing. Now it's real.

You might be worried about something else. Maybe your fear isn't failing. What if you take the step to get vulnerable, and when you tell people your goals they actually do laugh, scoff, or call you a poser?

That's okay too. It's what happened to pro-snowboarder-turned-coffee-peddler Nick Visconti a few different times in his journey. At the age of sixteen his family moved four hours away from his childhood home in the Northern California Bay Area to the beautiful Sierra Nevada Mountains. Along with the views of Lake Tahoe, Nick also acquired lots of necessary outerwear and a new goal: he decided to become a professional snowboarder.

Sitting in plastic Adirondack chairs in the California mountain town or Truckee, Nick and I discussed his journey. He described his family as "supportive and loving, but not necessarily encouraging." And at an age where young adults often refine career choices, he went after something big, dangerous, and exclusive—not the trifecta most parents encourage.

Nick continued pursuing his dream, despite the fact that "nine of the ten people I told either couldn't or wouldn't help. But the one of ten who were helpful and encouraging was enough." That encouragement led to a twelve-year snowboarding career that included sponsors, ESPN articles, and headlining the final part for a major snowboarding movie.

After eight years traveling the world ripping and tearing, he began to set the stage for the next phase of his life. Volunteering at a local coffee shop, he learned everything about the coffee business. He heard from nine of ten people "Drink Coffee Do Stuff" was a stupid name for a coffee brand and he was bound for certain failure. But just like starting his snowboarding career, he had the one—the one of ten who gave him a chance, believed in him, and did everything they could to help him pursue his dream.

Another eight years has passed, Drink Coffee Do Stuff has three shops encircling Lake Tahoe and dozens of retail locations. It's not about proving people wrong; it's about pursuing your dreams, opening up to people, verbalizing what you are going to do. And if they don't believe you, that's okay. You're not telling them for *them*, you're telling them for *you*. You're telling them to give *it* power and turn your dream to a goal.

Back to the three-step protocol WIN. By turning your thoughts into words, you turn your dreams into goals. You give *it* power. And it turns out, giving it power is exactly how it turns into reality.

After verbalizing it, you've completed step one. In the coming chapters we'll break down what I and N are. We'll cover the next steps and then dive into tips and tricks to turn your dreams into goals and goals into reality.

Now go win your next hour!

Win Your Next Hour

Each chapter will end with a literal call to action. I am calling you to action. Don't skip these! Take a few minutes and practice winning your next hour.

Right now, before you turn the page, who can you tell your dreams to? Send a text or make a call and turn your dream into your goal.

CHAPTER 2

YOUR PRISON

It's paralyzing and uncomfortable. You're not alone; everyone gets that same feeling. Some people call it butterflies, nerves, or anxiety. You want to move forward, but it's so overwhelming. And that's when the procrastination parade begins.

You're sitting there in your Tommy Bahama lawn chair and the first float passes—a reminder that you can start next month when you have more time. Up next is the junior high school marching band's mis-keyed notes, a reminder you're not good enough to do it. The revving motors of the classic cars scream, "You don't have enough money."

You tell yourself it's not procrastinating and these are all legitimate reasons, but deep down you know the truth: every problem is solvable. The real reason is you're scared to start—scared of failure, and equally scared of success.

You're stuck in your own prison of comfort and identity.

"Most of the world lives in a state of mediocrity," according to Mario Lanzarotti. "It creates a sense of safety."[1]

Our lives are built around our current state. Your friends, family, job, and community are all connected to the current you. What does that mean for your identity if you change?

"Most of us are more afraid of our light than our darkness," Lanzarotti continued. "If you're overweight, the chances are many people you know are overweight."[2] Even if you don't like what you see in the mirror, it's what you're accustomed to. Like it or not, it's how your friends and family know you. Stepping outside of that is unknown and feels unsafe.

What happens if you begin a weight loss journey and succeed? Will your current friends still want to hang out with you if you don't want to binge drink and eat Cheetos on the couch every day?

Writing for *Psychology Today*, leadership development specialist Peter Bregman says, "We procrastinate on that big project precisely *because* it's important. So important, in fact, that we're too scared to work on it."[3]

Instead of facing that fear, we push it down. You hate your job and want to go back to school and finish your degree, but the process of change is scary, so you don't start. You're not happy with your current situation, but it's more comfortable than the unknown that is change. And it's miserable because you know "I'll start when..." means never starting. Because you'll keep moving the goal post and waiting for the perfect time that will never come.

If only you could be like them—the people you look up to who have done big things. The people who finished their graduate degree and got the career you want. The people who have written dozens of books. If only you were as brave as them.

The truth is everyone struggles with the same things you're going through. Everyone gets paralyzed by their fear. In his autobiographic book *On Writing*, famous author Stephen King says, "The scariest moment is always just before you start. After that, things can only get better."[4] That's where you need to look—on the other side of starting.

The best way to get there? Force action.

You can force action through a massive commitment. Make a commitment so big that the pain of failure seems larger than the fear of change. Moving across the country or a large financial outlay are amazingly effective motivational triggers.

Motivation Starts with Commitment

As I discussed motivation with Olympian Wes Kitts, it was moving 2,452 miles.

When Wes' college football career was over, he wasn't sure what to do next. Graduating from college is a big change for everyone, and for athletes, it's even bigger. The end of high-level competition leaves a crater in your self-identity. Some athletes begin coaching to fill the void, others find a new pursuit in a different sport.

For Wes, that other sport was Olympic-style weightlifting. And after a few short years, it was becoming increasingly obvious he had the potential to be a much better weightlifter than he was football player. He could be the best in the country. With the right coaching, program, team, and training, he could be the best in the world.

All the missing pieces were available to him in California, but there was a catch. His life was in Knoxville, Tennessee. He had begun laying down roots by opening a gym and getting engaged in the same year. As his success in weightlifting grew, he had to make a decision. If he was going to chase that crazy dream—the Olympics—he would need to force massive action.

He made a decision that had consequences far beyond the fear of change. Three months before his wedding, he moved across the country to California where his fiancé would join him after their nuptials.

"There wasn't a lot waiting for me when I got out to California Strength," Wes recalled during our conversation. "After moving my wife out here away from our families and friends, I had to give it everything."

Four Pan American gold medals, a few American records, and top ten finishes in two Olympic Games were the result. And none of it would have happened without committing to something that made backing down more painful than following through.

Moving across the country is a vote for your future and believing in yourself. For Wes, relocating his life was his way of taking major action. But one can spur action in many ways. While studying for his PhD, author Benjamin Hardy interviewed entrepreneurs and wannabe entrepreneurs. One question separated the two groups clearly: "Have you ever had a 'point-of-no-return' experience?"[5]

Although the wannabes alluded to hoping to have a point-of-no-return experience at some juncture, nearly all of the successful entrepreneurs said yes and were able to point to multiple experiences throughout different stages of their growth and success.

Hardy went on to explain that "what often created a point-of-no-return experience was making a financial investment in the goal."[6]

You might remember my favorite barista-turned-business owner Erica from the last chapter. When Erica told me she decided to leave her job and open a mobile coffee trailer, she took major action. Knowing she wanted to start a mobile coffee shop, she bought a trailer—not a ready-to-go coffee shop on wheels, but a regular enclosed trailer like my landscaper uses. She had a vision of what it would look like after the transformation from hauling lawnmowers to serving lattes was complete.

Purchasing the trailer was a commitment. In her driveway, it was a daily reminder of what her future looked like. It was also a reminder of the money she had spent on it.

Starting her journey by purchasing the trailer forced her forward. The financial outlay took the dream in her mind and turned it into a goal in the real world. And since the trailer was a big, physical thing, it also forced her to talk about her goals with family, friends, and the stranger she bought it from. When they asked what it was for, she told them, "I'm going to turn it into a coffee shop." This one purchase helped her with two steps of the WIN protocol! She had to use her words and made an investment.

But the financial commitment doesn't have to be an eyesore in the driveway. It just has to put you in a position where the risk of loss is scarier and more motivating than the fear of starting. I've seen this recurring theme in my life as well. We had an idea, a dream. How much fun would that be? The plan wasn't to launch a business. We just wanted to host an event.

The Point of No Return

The goal: get the best weightlifters in the country to fly to Sacramento and compete head to head in an invitation only weightlifting meet for the biggest cash prize in modern weightlifting. The problem: We needed a venue, money for the cash prize, and athletes to commit.

Before talking to sponsors about the cash prize, we needed committed athletes. Before convincing athletes to interrupt their training and fly to California we needed an event date. Before announcing an event date, we needed a venue. To book a venue, we needed a deposit. We weren't a company with funding—just three guys who wanted to turn this dream into a goal, and then into reality.

The first venue we walked through was perfect. It had enough space for the stage, seating, and competition floor. The only issue? The seven-thousand-dollar deposit.

I did the math in my head to see if this could work. If we run a CrossFit-style team competition during the day and the invitation weightlifting meet at nights, it could work. At four hundred dollars per team, we would only need eighteen teams to cover that expense. With our connections in town, I was certain we could blow that number out of the water. It was a no-brainer!

I pulled out my wallet and handed over my credit card.

Because I had conviction in that moment, it didn't seem like a risk. It was clearly the path forward. We now had ten weeks to make it happen, or I'd have to explain to my wife why I spent seven thousand dollars on an event venue without discussing it first, which was not a conversation I wanted to have. That was motivation at its highest level.

As weightlifters committed to the event, we got a sponsor for the cash prize. Teams began signing up, and the buzz around the event resulted in people demanding event merch before it even started. The event turned into an online store, and the seven thousand dollars turned into a business that generated over fifteen million in revenue.

"It all starts with a financial investment," said Hardy. "It all starts with shifting your story and shifting your identity."[7]

The financial commitment forces you to make the shift from someone who has a dream, to someone who has a goal. You who has skin in the game. You become a person who is taking action and is no longer scared of success but *needs* to succeed. It's a vote for the person you want to become.

For the last four years, I've wanted to write a book. Spending the lion's share of my free time reading, studying, and practicing self-improvement and business over the last decade, I often found myself an outlet of advice for others. People started asking for some tips and tricks when they were starting something new or ran into a wall. It started with friends and acquaintances and turned to strangers reaching out through social media. It was invigorating helping people accomplish their dreams! I couldn't shake the thought of helping more people. I needed a way to scale what fired me up and helped others take action.

But it was just an idea, just a dream. What took me so long to take action? I kept kicking the can down the road with small actions that barely budged the needle forward—small actions that felt like I was doing something, but nothing that would put forty thousand words on paper. I read and studied half a dozen books on writing to improve my skills. I started a weekly email blog to practice writing. I did some half-ass online research about self-publishing versus shopping a book around.

It was enough action to make me feel like I was working toward it, but not enough to scare me. Not enough to pull me out of my comfort zone and make me change my self-identity. The fear and uncertainty were driving my procrastination.

What forced me to start? Ten thousand dollars.

After Angela told me about the course she took that led her through the book writing process, she sent me the professor's information. I hopped on a call with him to explore the course and see if it was a fit. We discussed ideas, the value of information, and whether I actually had a book to write.

As our call wrapped up, I was encouraged. He believed in me, and I began to believe I actually *could* do it. Then, the price of the course was revealed.

This became the inflection point for me. I believed the course could help me turn my dream into a goal and into reality. But saying I believed it and committing to it are different things. I knew paying for the course would force action.

So, I did it. I paid ten thousand dollars and signed up for the course. As soon as I did, I actually felt relief instead of fear. The only way I would get that money back was by finishing the book and selling it. I didn't look at the ten thousand dollars as an expense, but as a loan. An investment to yield massive returns. Through book sales, events, workshops, and speaking gigs, I'll recoup the ten thousand dollars many of times over.

And one thing is absolute: as a result of paying ten thousand dollars, I would finish this book on time and release it. The financial investment in my goal was motivating. It was my point-of-no-return experience that took me from kicking the can down the road with inconsequential tasks, to getting serious and taking massive action.

Hardy explained how a financial outlay forces action by helping you truly commit: "100% commitment is easier than 98%."[8]

We've all experienced that in our lives. It's easier to have zero pieces of candy than to just have one. It's easier to get up early every day than to make a decision about hitting the snooze button each morning. This is why you have to force action. Make an investment of time or money that will plunge you into "all in" territory. The land of 100 percent commitment.

When you have to make the decision every day to stick to your plan, you get decision fatigue. Your willpower slowly falls off and following through becomes exhausting. The "I'll call him tomorrow" bug burrows in your ear. You can avoid that with 100 percent commitment. You don't have to make the decision in the moment because you already made it a month ago.

This morning, I didn't really want to write. After a busy weekend that involved a few too many adult beverages, pushing my alarm back an hour sounded fantastic. All the justifications were there: I had a busy day, I needed to be well rested to perform my best, and sleep was very important for productivity.

Although those may be true, skipping a day would put me behind pace. All day, I would have this stress hanging over my head knowing I was falling behind. And the biggest thing? I really didn't have the opportunity to even make the decision. The decision was made seven weeks ago when I paid for the course. I have a meeting with my editor in three days, and I need to have another 2,500 words completed before then. The investment I made forced one hundred percent commitment. The decision was already made.

When people accomplish goals—the coffee cart is finished and dealing out espresso shots, the book launches, you qualify for the Olympics—it often seems like the recent win is what made it happen. It's natural to celebrate the final steps like getting a business license, launching the book with a release party, or lifting the winning weight in competition. Although these are the things you see and celebrate, those moments are just consequences of previous actions. Accomplishing your goal requires a series of wins you can follow back like a trail of breadcrumbs to where you started.

In retrospect, you'll notice the winning move was rarely the last action. So take pride and be excited for the small steps along the way, not knowing if it will have been the linchpin activity. For many, that clutch action is the investment—which is why the next step in the protocol WIN is investment. You must make an investment in yourself and your goal to force action.

And the secret sauce to the WIN protocol? Stack them up and let them build together. When you're telling people about your dream which has turned to a goal, make sure to tell them what's on the line. When someone else knows how much you're invested in your goal, that will add another layer of responsibility.

I did not want to squander ten thousand dollars. That investment turned this project into an eight-out-of-ten priority. Telling my wife how much I spent on the course turned it into a nine-out-of-ten priority. That is how you raise the stakes! If I didn't follow through, not only would I be out a significant amount of cash, but my wife would know I wasted our hard-earned money. I would be a bad investment, which I cannot let happen.

What massive action can you take to force your hand? How can you create a point of no return that will thrust you into action?

Is your goal to move to a different city? Put your house up for sale.

Is your goal to lose weight? Join an expensive gym and pay for one year in advance.

Is your goal to start a business? Lease the building, buy the equipment, or enroll in the top training program.

If you're struggling to know where to start, use this brainstorming method: ten ideas.

Ten Ideas to Force Action and Invest in Your Dreams

Sit down with actual paper and pen and number one to ten down the left column. Now, don't get up until you have written down ten ideas for how you can invest in your goal. Can you take a course or hire a coach? Maybe you book a flight or sign up for a conference.

Ideas one, two, and three will come pretty quickly and easily. Good! That's part of why this works. Write down the first few already floating around in your mind. Ideas four, five, and six will take a few minutes, but you can get them down in a reasonable time. Generally, next is where you'll get stuck. You'll think you got all the best ideas down, but stick with it! Ideas seven, eight, and nine are usually where the magic happens—the ideas that are another layer down, buried beneath your preconceived thoughts you've been focused on. Idea ten usually sucks...but that's okay. Write down some outlandish shit, and see where it goes.

Your ten ideas brainstorm is a great way to win your next hour! Use your next hour to make your list, and then pick the idea that will force action.

Make the commitment. Commit yourself to the task by taking one small action, right now. You can accomplish your goal by choosing to bank a small win that forces massive action.

So what are you going to do? How will you create your "point-of-no-return" moment? Get in over your head and figure it out.

Win Your Next Hour

Brainstorm ten ideas on how you can invest in your goal. Is there a course you can buy? A program to sign up for? A place you can book travel to? Make a list, and pick the one that will get you the closest to your goal and make the consequences of quitting unbearable.

CHAPTER 3

YOUR DEATH SENTENCE

Jeff Lund explained to me that he couldn't believe it had already been ten years.

After growing up pulling fish out of the rushing rivers of Alaska, Jeff now lived in California's central valley. He'd landed here after college temporarily and had never intended to make this place home. What had started off as something to do for a year or two while figuring it out, had turned into an entire decade of knowing he wanted to live somewhere else, and waiting—a decade of knowing he wasn't living his purpose, but instead putting his head down and making the most of his situation.

And the crazy thing? He knew better. He had grown up living an example of making a bold move to try something new.

When he was five, his parents, both teachers in Ordway, Colorado, were presented with an opportunity and moved their family to a remote island in Alaska to start a new adventure.

Alaska was in desperate need of teachers. Ranking forty-nine out of fifty states in college educated residents, teachers needed to be imported to fill the small schools spread around the massive territory. Given the harshness of frigid winters inland, and remoteness of islands around the edges, Alaska needed to motivate teachers to move in. Financial incentives worked, but only on those willing to take a chance and go on an adventure.

Uprooting everything, the Lunds moved their family 1,805 miles to Prince of Wales Island in Southeast Alaska. After long miles behind the wheel, the trip required a three-hour ferry to reach their new home where they joined the island population of just five thousand residents.

Jeff's childhood changed drastically. In Ordway, his house had a cement driveway and fenced in backyard. Mornings before school were now filled with walking to the river to catch a few salmon before the first bell rang. Evenings after school involved float planes to "nearby" islands for basketball games. He recalled an eye-opening experience that made it very clear they weren't in Colorado anymore. Loading into a series of float planes, two brothers were stopped by the basketball coach as they boarded. Siblings were not allowed to be in the same six-seater airplane. When they asked their coach why, he raised his eyebrows and took a deep breath. Before he began, the boys nodded with the realization that the school policy prevented parents from losing *both* their children in the event of an emergency.

As time went on, the Lunds gained experience in the Alaska life. Hiking, fishing, and eating what you caught instead of what you bought became their new normal—and they loved it.

Jeff admitted graduating third in his class of sixteen students "looks awesome on transcripts, until you see how many kids there were." Leaving nature's playground to attend the University of Arizona, he was one of just three students from his high school to pursue a college education.

After graduating with a journalism degree, Jeff was looking for the next step. His roommate was moving back home to Manteca, a small town in California's central valley, to pursue teaching. The school he landed at needed an English teacher, so he called Jeff. And that's how a boy who grew up fishing for thirty-two-pounds salmon in Alaska ended up in a California farming community.

It was temporary. Just until he found where he wanted to live. Just until he could move to somewhere that had more fish than cows. But ten years later, he was still surrounded by the sweet smell of manure.

He had friends who were fun, colleagues he liked, and a rewarding job. And every summer he would drive to the airport the first day of summer break, heading home to Alaska. Spending every day fishing, hiking, and living the Alaska dream, he would return back to California the day before the first bell rang on the first day of school.

"It was the snowbird lifestyle." Jeff loved that he "could go play all summer and be back in California to avoid the harsh Alaska winters." He had set down some roots, including a weekly outdoors column in the local newspaper where he would document his summers of conquest and weekends of glory.

But Manteca was never meant to be a decade-long stop. He made the best of it, but knew it wasn't where he ultimately wanted to be.

Jeff often talked about moving somewhere different, but it was comfortable in Manteca. Admittedly, he had a good thing going. But, as parents age, situations change. After his mom's second aneurism in the span of a few years, Jeff felt compelled to go home and care for her.

"For me, it was a heart choice more than a head decision or gut feeling," Lund remembered. He had no choice, so as soon as school let out he moved back home to Alaska. This move, too, at first was temporary. He settled back into his childhood bedroom, planning to return to Manteca in time for the next school year. Then something happened.

An English teaching job opened in Ketchikan, a short three-hour ferry ride away from his home island and his mom. This was it, the time to make the decision. He could head back to California, to a life he enjoyed, but one that limited his options. Or he could go for it. Take the leap into a new chapter. One with colder winters, but also alpine peaks to hunt for mountain goats. One with more rain, but also more salmon to catch in the rivers and ocean. One with fewer people, but more outdoor experiences for his writing.

It may sound like an easy decision, but look at your own life. Many of us see all the positives and opportunities of going after *it*. But opportunities and unknowns travel together. Every opportunity involves the risk that it won't work out. It takes courage to go after your dreams.

Jeff took the job and the accompanying opportunity to live in his summer playground.

Regret would not be a part of his life.

The Courage to Live

For many, regret is a part of their death.

Bronnie Ware was an Australian palliative care professional. In her memoir The *Top Five Regrets of Dying,* she recalled her years of caring for the dying and the hard lessons she learned along the way. Through her experiences, the number one regret expressed by passing patients was "I wish I'd had the courage to live a life true to myself."[1]

Often, you'll find yourself scared, paralyzed by the fear of failure. But what you should be fearful of is not trying, which will lead to living your last days with regret. The worst that can happen is you fail, and that's something we all do.

During those failures, you learn what doesn't work. What a blessing! You can then try a different path and use the lessons learned to manufacture wins.

The problem arises in that first step—courage. In her book *The Courageous Mind*, Angela Schroeder offers the advice, "[C]ourage comes before confidence. Before we have confidence in a skill set...that we can succeed at something, we must choose courage first."[2] You must feel the fear and choose to act anyway. That action will build confidence in yourself.

It took massive amounts of courage for the Lund family to decide to uproot their family and move to Alaska to start a new adventure. They left behind friends, a community, and steady jobs. Thirty years later when Jeff moved back to Alaska, it took that same courage. Pushing aside the fear of the unknown, they took action. They followed where their hearts led them and left behind the prison of comfort and certainty.

Words like "courage," "confidence," and "bravery" can feel like traits some people are born with or learn at an early age. But the truth is it's never too late. They are traits that are learned and earned through choices and actions. You can be courageous and confident. Train yourself to take action in a way that develops those traits.

Win Your Next Twenty Seconds

In her TEDx Talk, Emily Jaenson provided a framework for building confidence, and therefore courage. As a woman, being the general manager of a professional baseball team came with many challenges. Among those are imposter syndrome and a long line of overwhelming obligations. When faced with a daunting task, she would ask herself, "What if I only have to be brave for twenty seconds?"[3]

Twenty-seconds is a timeframe we can stomach. You can do anything for just twenty seconds—enough time to push a button, dial a phone number, or walk in that door. It can be the first third of the first minute of your next hour you set out to win.

If you're not sure what to do in those twenty seconds, Jaenson has a tip: "How does the person I want to become behave?"[4]

Although this advice sounds like the common adage "fake it 'til you make it," it's slightly different.

Jaenson went on to explain, "To get people to change, you need to not start with the attitudes, but with the behaviors associated with those attitudes."[5] If you want to be more confident, you can't simply adopt the attitude of confidence. But you can mimic the behaviors of one who is confident. You can act on this premise: what would a confident person do in this situation?

As you collect twenty second moments of courage and practice acting confident, you're proving a point to yourself. Your acts of bravery are real, which is a win. Enrolling in the course, hiring the coach, buying the trailer, moving across the country—these are all wins.

And winning begets winning because it builds confidence. In her book *Confidence*, Rosabeth Moss Kanter describes how the confidence from small wins takes you from "praying to win, to expecting to win."[6]

That expectation of winning is called confidence, and it creates a virtuous loop of courage, learning, application, and success.

Momentum builds, winning begets winning, and you must celebrate your wins. Jaenson arrived at the epiphany, "Confidence is born in all we've already done and already achieved."[7] Think about your proudest moments and what you're really good at. Use the strength from those memories and corral them together with your twenty second wins that lead to winning your next hour.

You hear the advice, "Enjoy the process," but it's usually coming from someone who's already accomplished the goal. It's the winning quarterback's word vomit after winning the big game. Cynically, we think how it's easy to say after the goal is accomplished. But what does "the process" actually entail?

It's a series of trials and errors, trials and successes. It's a practice of repeating success until it becomes expected. Enjoying the process really means celebrate your small wins while preparing for the big win.

2902.4 Miles

Louis Chaix told me about being bloodied in a ditch on the side of the road, just twelve days into his eighty-day challenge to skate across the country. The people he was relying on to help were beginning to doubt. They advised him to "take a day off," but he knew what he really needed was the opposite. He needed to double—or even triple—down. He *had* set out to skate across America, and days off would make it impossible. He *had* to do it. He had to do it for the kids.

Louis was only six years old when one day his entire body began to burn. Feeling like his skin was on fire, the rash began to spread. Soon, ninety percent of his little body was covered in a rash. And the damage to his brain and body beneath the surface was worsening as well.

Weeks passed, and the doctors still had no answer for Louis or his parents. Their child was burning from the inside out, and there was nothing they could do.

After an emergency transfer to a bigger city with more resources, Louis was diagnosed with an extreme case of Stevens Johnson syndrome, known as toxic epidermal necrolysis (TEN). The affliction cause is widely unknown, but often linked to an adverse reaction to medications such as antibiotics. It's entirely possible that the previous weeks in the hospital had been making him worse. With 90 percent of his body covered in second degree burns and a 50 percent survival rate, the six-year-old had a battle in front of him.

The doctors prepared his parents for the worst-case scenario—losing their little boy to the syndrome. They knew hope and belief would help Louis fight and make it through. To give Louis hope, his father bought him a brand-new hockey kit. One he could use when he got out of the hospital and learned to walk and skate again. Over the next few weeks Louis improved little by little, every day. Those days turned to weeks and months. After two years, Louis could skate again and put the unused hockey kit to use.

It was three years before Louis was allowed to go out in the sun. His days were filled with physical therapy—learning to walk before returning to the ice. He had to relearn basic skills he had previously perfected as a toddler.

As he got older, his hockey skills improved and Louis became a leader on his team. He wanted to make hockey his career and knew he had to go where the action was. After everything he'd been through, his parents couldn't say no to letting him live out his dream. At the age of fifteen, Louis moved away from his family to Canada to pursue a career in hockey. Living with host families in North America, he excelled in his new environment and eventually was recruited to play the sport he loved in college.

During his senior year of college, Louis was playing hockey at Missouri State University when he had an idea. What if he could roller blade across America? It was a massive dream and one he could use to raise awareness for his rare childhood disease, which struggles to acquire funding due to lack of awareness. Louis knew if he could document his journey skating across America, that would get people's attention. That attention would help raise funds, which would help save the lives of others suffering with TEN. Leaning on a friend who knew an experienced documentary filmmaker, he jumped into training and planning. He had to be more fit than he ever imagined possible, and more organized than ever.

Louis explained, "Once I figured out the starting date, I had to wait until after hockey season was over to protect my body. Then I trained for six months, six days a week for six to eight hours per day, on top of school and working construction."

He knew he had 180 days until he would fly to Venice Beach in California to begin the 2,902.4-mile trek to Times Square. After each day of training, he changed the number on his mirror.

Day one. Day two. Day three.

Each day he trained he was another day closer. Each day closer he updated his countdown on the mirror. Each day he wrote down his progress, he gained confidence. He proved to himself he would do what he promised. He would skate across America, and more kids would survive TEN.

On the same day Louis was pulled from the ditch with all the skin ripped off both shins, the producer behind the documentary they were filming for the project pulled him aside and warned they'd run out of funding soon— twenty days short of New York.

The prospect of not finishing drove Louis to push harder. The next day he skated ninety-four miles, nearly double his previous longest day. He felt unstoppable after seeing what he was capable of.

With this new momentum, he started changing his approach. Remembering how good it felt to change the day on the mirror during his training months, Louis began to focus on smaller milestones. He went from skating fifty-five miles a day, to skating in twenty-five-mile blocks. Sometimes he would cover forty miles in an hour, and sometimes he would walk through gravel in his skates. But he always reminded himself, "Tonight I'll be sleeping in my bed." He just had to get through his next twenty-five miles. He just had to win his next hour.

Louis knew the power of tracking small wins and progress. He looked back at his journey and lessons learned. "It showed me you can do whatever you want, if you just start and track your progress."

Forty-five days, ten hours, and forty-four seconds after pushing off in California, Louis arrived in Times Square, setting a world record.

Louis' story is one of perseverance and courage. His childhood affliction taught him to go after his dreams and take on big challenges one day at a time. Noting his progress gave him the courage to keep going.

The Power List

For Louis, noting progress meant markers on the mirror. But you can manufacture motivation in another way if you don't have a hard start date.

Here's a practice I dive into when it's time to buckle down and drive forward. I use the Power List, which I learned from entrepreneur and podcaster Andy Frisella. The Power List is similar to a to-do list but has one major difference which can change your life. Andy explains in episode 107 of his podcast *The MFCEO Project* you need to write down "critical tasks that will move you forward. We're not talking about 'brush your teeth,' unless brushing your teeth is a problem for you."[8]

And here's the secret sauce: you don't get any roll-over tasks.

Each day you write down five must-do tasks. Cross them off as you go, and after you accomplish them all write a big "W" on the page. The "W" is to signify you won the day. It's a win you can get every day.

When you're making the list, your tasks need to be process oriented. It's not a goal list, it's a tasks list. "These are things you can actually do," Frisella explained. It's not "I'll make a million dollars"; it's "Call _____ to discuss the business proposition."[9] They are things you can control, tasks that push the needle forward. They are not dependent on other people. You are taking responsibility for yourself and your own actions.

Attack the list with the goal of winning your next one hundred days undefeated. One hundred-zero. This isn't little league; there is no mercy rule. You need to set out to dominate one hundred successive days.

That is how you build confidence. Even if you drop a few days and end up ninety-ten, that is still ninety wins in one hundred days. And that is a win. That's how winning and losing works; if you scored more points, you won!

This is a tool I use whenever I'm feeling overwhelmed, unproductive, or scared. In fact, I started a new one-hundred-day Power List when I began writing this book. I have two children in elementary school and two businesses I'm involved in daily. The holiday season is hectic. Between Black Friday weekend and school holiday plans with the family, it's probably not the best time to have an elbow surgery and begin writing a book.

But I know the time will never be right. If I wait until the new year, I will have other challenges, which will push the project back to the summer. And the summer is when my work travel schedule kicks up, which would push the book to fall. September through November is when the Caffeine and Kilos Invitational and other events back home require my attention.

If I ever want to turn my dream of writing a book in a goal, I need to start now. And the only way to not have my life fall apart is to Power List my way to success. I get all the important stuff done, and feel the wins stack up every day. Writing that "W" on the page day after day builds my confidence and encourages me to keep going.

This brings us to "N" in the WIN protocol. "N" is for "note your progress." By keeping track of your progress, your courage will turn to confidence, and you will feel your goal getting closer day after day.

The WIN protocol:

W—Words
I—Investment
N—Note Progress

Use words to talk to other people and to yourself! Say your goals out loud to make them real. Invest your time, money, and energy into your goal. Create for yourself a point of no return where failure is not an option. Then keep track of your wins and progress somewhere physically. Mark off days on a calendar, your bathroom mirror, or in your Power List.

Follow the WIN protocol, and your dreams will turn into goals and your goals into reality.

Now you have the recipe for success, but you still need to execute. You need to know what steps to take and how to climb them day in and day out. How do you keep building and keep your momentum going? How do you persevere when it gets hard? In the next chapters, we'll look at how you can keep going when you feel like you hit a wall and want to quit.

Win Your Next Hour

It's time for action. How can you note your progress? It's time for you to start tracking your wins. Go buy a cheap one-hundred-page notebook, a new calendar to X off days, or a fresh marker for the mirror. Start recording your progress to build confidence and become the person who has courage to start.

CHAPTER 4

WINNING STREAKS

Cory Gregory grew up in a single wide trailer where if he spilled something in the kitchen, he had to clean splash marks off the living room couch. His mom worked long hours as a waitress at the local buffet to squeeze out the 150-dollar monthly rent payment. His grandfather, uncle, and father were coal miners.

That was his lineage, his destiny. As a fourth-generation coal miner, he would work in the mine for back-to-back sixteen-hour shifts until one of two things happened: he developed an opioid addiction while coping with back problems from working in a tunnel less than forty inches tall, or died in the tunnel from a collapse, gas leak, or explosion. All with the hopes of being able to move to a double-wide trailer where spilled milk could only reach the other side of the kitchen.

But Cory wanted more. From a young age, he felt like he was destined for something bigger. But what? And how?

In high school, it was hard to imagine a better life when he had to get in a beat-up Plymouth Horizon through the backseat because the driver-side door didn't have a handle. What kept his dream alive was the one thing money can't buy: passion. He loved working out and how it made him feel. He saw the positives it brought to his life and the lives of others. Wanting to help people experience that, he dreamt of a job as a personal trainer. However, he faced a problem with that pursuit: where he grew up, it wasn't possible.

Nobody in his hometown of Amsterdam, Ohio, had even heard of that job. People paying you to make them work hard and get sweaty? Sounded silly to a community that busted their asses sixteen hours a day, six days a week just to put canned food on the table. But Cory was obsessed with the idea. He studied fitness training daily and did not miss a training day in the gym.

He went to the library every day to study the magazines about training. *Muscle & Fitness* magazine was the only thing he read for the entire four years of high school. When his friends were getting ready to move to Columbus to attend Ohio State University, Cory didn't have the grades or the funds to join them. Their way out of town could not be his. As he looked for a way out, a way to pursue something bigger than the hand he was dealt, he found something. A junior college in Columbus offered a personal training certification course.

This was his chance to get out of the town that had trapped so many before him. He had dreams of doing something bigger: helping people. But first he needed to do more than just survive another day six-hundred-feet underground in Tunnel 7A. He needed enough money to fund a few months of bare bones living expenses and his share of the deposit on the apartment in Columbus.

After high school, he went all in on his dream. Cory took a job in the coal mines and worked like a mad man for six months. The wage for his standard sixteen-hour shift wasn't that great, but overtime pay was worth shoveling coal from his knees while his back scraped the top of the tunnel. Cory took every opportunity to head straight back in the hole for consecutive shifts to make the overtime wages. A few breaths of fresh air, and then back into the darkness on a ninety-minute ride to his workstation shoveling on his knees. He went underground every shift possible and did not miss a day of work.

Stacking every dollar from eighty-hour work weeks, he moved to Columbus and became a personal trainer. That led him to opening a small gym—one where if you spilled a protein shake by the treadmills you would have to clean it off the bathroom door.

Meeting people in the fitness space, he made some connections and started a supplement company. His dedication to training and success led him to features on the cover of his high school reading material—*Muscle & Fitness* magazine. The magazine covers eventually led him to become friends and business partners with the biggest name in fitness, Arnold Schwarzenegger. That relationship fueled his supplement company to explosive growth.

Cory's life now looks different. During our interview, Cory told me he had just bought an island. The single wide trailer he grew up in would look like a tiny home short-term rental on his five-acre estate just two hours from where he grew up. And the driver-side door on his Rolls Royce has a working handle.

When discussing his successes, Gregory insisted he isn't special. Nothing he does is special, except one thing. "I just don't fucking miss," he explained. He unapologetically follows his dreams, and when he makes a commitment, he shows up every day. And that streak of small wins gives him the confidence to attack each opportunity he sees.

Cory's heaviest workload in Tunnel 7A was a ninety-three-hour week. "I can't remember taking any days off in the mine." But even in the hardest work weeks, he stayed consistent with his training.

"I haven't missed more than a week's workout since I was a sophomore in high school. I fell in love with my process."

His winning streaks are epic. Four hundred meters of walking lunges for two hundred consecutive days when he needs to get lean for a photo shoot. Heavy squats every day when he needs to build size and strength for powerlifting competitions. He's recorded a daily workout video for his online clients every day for three years. Cory explained, "When I would string together days and get the results, it built confidence."

His success is a product of hard work and consistency. He shows up daily and doesn't miss. Winning streaks are one of the most powerful tools you have to create winning habits, build confidence, and turn your goals into reality.

James Clear promotes the power of streaks in his book *Atomic Habits: An Easy & Proven Way to Build New Habits & Break Bad Ones*. Clear explains that creating a streak of small wins make it easy to create new habits. And those new habits make up your daily actions.

"Every action you take is a vote for the type of person you wish to become," says Clear in his book.[1]

If you want to run a marathon, you need to take the actions of someone who runs marathons. You need to build the habits of a runner. What does a marathon runner do? They don't miss their training workouts.

Clear goes on to explain, "The first mistake is never the one that ruins you. It is the spiral of repeated mistakes that follows. Missing once is an accident. Missing twice is the start of a new habit."[2]

How does he recommend you don't miss twice? Don't rely on discipline. Instead, create a steady habit that is so easy to follow through on that it happens almost effortlessly.

Break the task down into steps that are so small you don't even think about missing. Tasks you aren't intimidated to try. Make it so simple you don't have to convince yourself to follow through.

To further increase your chances of success, remove all friction. Put the clothes you're going to wear next to your bed. Take your running shoes and put them in front of the first chair you usually sit in. Get the coffee grounds in the filter and water in the coffee pot so it's ready to pour. The night before day one, remove anything that can be used as an excuse or inconvenience.

The plan is to set up a slippery slope of micro-habits you can cruise down without any decisions. Remove forks in the road. Make the right decision the easiest step to take.

While discussing his book, James explained to me, "In many cases it's not 'what do I look like on my best days,' but 'what can I stick to on my bad days?'" He went on to explain the best way to begin your new habits is to "reduce the scope, but always stick to the schedule. We get so wrapped up in what the perfect version looks like, when all you really need to do is show up."

If you currently don't run at all, making the plan to run five miles every morning is a fool's errand. Should you make running one mile a day the goal?

Start even smaller. If you currently run zero miles a day, let's work on getting out the door. For seven days set the goal to put on your running shoes and go outside. After seven days of success, roll that streak into a streak of seven days of jogging one lap around the block. That's it. Just one lap around the block. Then run one lap followed by walking a second lap for seven days.

Now that you've built up twenty-one days of putting on your running shoes and getting out the door, you'll find it becomes automatic. The internal struggle of tying your shoes and hitting the road is gone. Now it's your habit. Your daily vote for the type of person you want to be.

You must establish a pattern of success, then build from there.

The Winning Streak Builds Confidence

Charlie Rocket was three hundred pounds and battling a brain tumor when he decided he wanted more out of his life. Instead of laying down and accepting his life was coming to an end, he decided to start winning. Taking massive action, Charlie signed up for a triathlon and got to work. He looked at every positive in his life as a win and used that momentum to build winning streaks. In his talk "Delusional Optimist (How to Start a Winning Streak)," he explains, "When we simply see the wins, we feel like a winner. And when you feel like a winner, you start expecting to win."[3]

That expectation of winning is called *confidence.*

The secret sauce to success is starting. The secret ingredient to the secret sauce is confidence. The way to build confidence is by trusting yourself. You earn trust by making promises and keeping them. It's the streak of wins, the chain of X's on a calendar, the consistent W's on your Power List that cause you to trust in yourself.

You trust yourself to follow through on promises and therefore have the confidence to start. The fear of failure is minimized because you believe in yourself.

When Cory Gregory's company Max Effort Muscle was navigating some challenging economic patterns he detailed a plan of attack in a letter to investors. I replied with just one statement: "You've got this, Cory. I believe in you."

His response was a single statement: "I believe in me too!"

And that's what a winning streak will also do for you. It will build your confidence to a level where you know you can do it. You've proven to yourself that you do what you say you will do. You are trustworthy. You have followed through.

The Winning Streak Makes Delayed Gratification Bearable

Achieving involves a dichotomy of struggle. The time it takes to accomplish big goals and the common advice to "enjoy the process" seem to be at odds. How can you enjoy the process when the end goal is still years away?

Big dreams and goals can take years to develop. It takes years to grow a business or to complete a college degree.

The ability to delay gratification is what creates high achievers. In his peer-reviewed journal article about increasing delay of gratification ability, John Protzko states children who can delay gratification "go to school for longer, have healthier bodyweights, (and) have higher academic achievement."[4]

But delaying gratification is hard, especially for goals that take years to develop. So how do you do it? When the payoff is years in the future, how do you enjoy the process while working toward a goal?

Enter your winning streak. An opportunity to have a win every day. An opportunity to celebrate every day. You can't do the big things unless you do the little things, because the big things are just a series of little things!

Mark Twain commented, "The secret of getting ahead is getting started. The secret of getting started is breaking your complex overwhelming tasks into small manageable tasks, and starting on the first one."[5]

This brings us to actually starting. So, how do you know where to start?

You start with the ten-item brainstorming list from chapter 2. Write down ten places you can start, and don't give up on your list until you get all ten. Pick one that seems the least intimidating and get to work! Make it a pattern of working on that single item, and celebrate your winning streak daily. It might be the wrong place to start. But that's okay! The fact that you started in the wrong place is actually a win! Let me explain.

Now you know where not to start next time. You'll learn from that experience, and for the rest of your life you'll make better choices about where to begin. Also, just because it's not the ideal place to start doesn't mean your plans are ruined. That's the power of winning streaks.

Some point in time, an experience or decision, will be the pivotal moment. The inflection point. But most often, you won't know what it is in real time. It's only in retrospect that you realize which of the dots you connected was the linchpin. It's only through reflection that you can connect the pivotal moments.

The only way to manufacture those pivotal moments is to take action consistently.

Asking for Help Is a Win

In August of 2010, I competed in my first weightlifting meet.

USA Weightlifting was experiencing exponential growth in memberships. As CrossFit gyms began popping up all over the country, more people were exposed to barbells and the competition lifts for Olympic style weightlifting. Capitalizing on the growth, USA Weightlifting and CrossFit teamed up in a cross-promotion by cohosting a competition. Hosted near the

Olympic training center in Colorado Springs, the event consisted of a sanctioned weightlifting meet, followed by one CrossFit style workout. The best combination of scores would determine the winner.

A few friends encouraged me to sign up. Although I had never competed in CrossFit or a weightlifting meet, it sounded like fun, so I registered. Looking back to chapter 2 and the "I" in WIN, I made the investment of registering for a competition that would require me to join USA Weightlifting, fly to Colorado, and stay in a hotel—all for something I had never done before. I was invested.

Since I had never competed in weightlifting, I decided to do a few local meets before flying 1,200 miles away for one. I signed up for competitions in August and September to prep for the meet in Colorado in October.

It was August, and I began to warm up in the back hallway of a high school auditorium in Sacramento, California. My session was set to begin in less than an hour, so I began with general joint mobility and ended by building up to my opening competition weight. But something was off. Out of the other fourteen athletes in my session, precisely zero of them were warming up.

I was left with a decision. I could continue, not sure what to do, and hope it worked out, or I could take action. I looked around and found someone who looked like they knew what they were doing. Walking up to the coach, I explained that it was my first meet and asked if she could help me prepare to take the stage. After a few questions about my opening attempts, she pointed to the chair by the warmup platform and told me to sit down and not to move until she told me to.

Taking control, she guided me through every warm-up attempt in the hallway and every competition attempt on the platform. I ended up making all six of my attempts! It was such a great experience I couldn't wait to do it again. This was good because I had already signed up for another meet the following month.

At the time, I was asking for help because the alternative was embarrassing myself when they called me to lift during the meet. Looking back, I see approaching the coach was a pivotal moment that affected the next decade of my life.

In October of 2019, I won a gold medal at the Masters World Cup.

Obviously, a lot happened over the nine years between registering for USA Weightlifting and winning the Masters World Cup. And during those nine years, I made a lot of decisions, met a lot of people, and stacked a lot of winning days. They seemed like nothing more than a series of decisions and actions. Looking back now, I can pinpoint dozens of moments like this one that shaped my life over that time.

You can feel the weight of some big decisions—the decisions that include a large financial outlay, or the meeting you've been fighting to get for months. You will also have the decisions that are flippant "screw it" moments. But as you look back, you'll find your trajectory changed because of both. And it's not always the obvious forks in the road. That's why creating winning streaks matter. Doing something now is always better than waiting.

I Need a Winning Streak!

Now, I'm in another situation where showing up consistently matters. Writing this book has a deadline. And now, just 30 percent of the way through, I've been facing an unscheduled challenge. There's never a convenient time for surgery, and this is no exception.

Four days ago, I had an old weightlifting injury to my left elbow repaired. And now, at 5:35 a.m., I'm typing while my stitches are busy sliding, catching, and pulling on the arm of this chair. As annoying as the tugging of stitches at five incision sites is, the throbbing joint and muscle soreness is the bigger problem.

I have to write 2,500 words a week to stay on track and get the greenlight from my publisher. If I don't hit the deadlines, the publisher will drop me and that door closes. Until now, that hasn't been an issue. I write eight hundred words a day Monday through Wednesday and meet with my editor on Thursday. Then Friday through Sunday, I can go back and make revisions. It's been a great schedule.

But now I can only get a few paragraphs down before my elbow starts to pair the throbbing with some sharp pains in the joint before the tingling in my fingers increases to total numbness. That trio of sensations makes it physically difficult to type. Although challenging, that's not the worst part.

It's the mental challenge. Hitting weekly word counts is a challenge when everything is going well. Each writing session takes over an hour as part of the process. Like warming up before a workout, you can't skip the first twenty to thirty minutes. Sitting down and starting isn't so bad, but it takes time to get your thoughts organized. Then, you need to stop thinking and just let the writing ooze out. It's the flow state where sentences just lead to one another without prior thought or filters. The key is to take the filters out and let your subconscious do the work.

And that's the catch.

It takes me the first thirty minutes to get down the first seventy words before it starts to happen. Over the next forty-five minutes, I can get down the next seven hundred words. But with my elbow, I can only type for twenty minutes before the throbbing kicks in, and doubt decides to keep the physical symptoms company.

Am I delaying my recovery process by pushing it too much? Am I getting enough rest for my elbow to heal, or am I prolonging the process by over-using the joint? Will I be able to hit my word count in these short bursts?

Does my writing suck since I can barely get into my writing flow?

What I need is some wins. What I need is a winning streak!

At this point, the goal of hitting eight hundred words in each session isn't practical. It's setting the bar so high that I'm intimidated to even start. Knowing the first seventy words will be wading through mud isn't so bad when you know the following thirty minutes will lead to a flow of seven hundred. But starting is a challenge when the first seventy words leads to numb fingers and throbbing joints.

I need an easier target for this week. A goal that will remove friction and be easy to start. For the next week, it's less important that I hit the 2,500 words, and more important that I don't skip days.

If I don't sit down and get a few words out, my routine will be changed and it'll be harder to restart the daunting task to weekly minimums. So this week, the goal is to get words on the page. I just have to start. And when the pain and inconvenience of typing becomes so distracting that I can't think clearly, I'll stop.

The goal is to keep the streak alive. I need to keep sitting down every day and putting words on the page, and as my elbow heals I'll ramp back up to stay on track.

One life lesson I learned through the decade of training to compete in weightlifting is this: the goal of the program is the follow the program. Sometimes it will be inconvenient, painful, and discouraging. However, that doesn't change what needs to be done. It's acceptable to dial back intensity, but you have to show up. By staying consistent you'll keep moving forward and winning one day at a time.

Win Your Next Hour

What habit can you form that makes working toward your goal nearly effortless? How many decisions can you remove to ensure follow through? Make a plan for the next seven days that is so easy you don't have the risk of failure. Start stacking wins and building your streak of W's.

CHAPTER 5

YOUR ROAD MAP

Craig Ballantyne was all alone in his apartment, clutching his chest and stumbling around in pain. It was New Year's Day of 2006, and after a long night of drinking, he had just gotten out of bed at noon. His heart was racing and his breaths shallow. He'd thought getting out of bed and moving around would distract him, but pacing around his apartment wasn't working. His chest wouldn't relax, his breathing couldn't calm, and his heart rate refused to slow.

Trudging down eight flights of stairs to the ground floor, he pushed out into the snowy streets of Toronto and hailed a cab. "Can you take me to the hospital please?" was all he could squeak out. Craig thought he was having a heart attack.

At thirty years old, his days were filled with twelve hours of work followed by a six-beer minimum at the pub. He had built up a thriving personal training business that had a waiting list to work with him. It was the early days of video on the internet, and Craig had an idea: he would do at-home workout videos and sell them nationwide. It was working, but it took every minute of daylight in the summer and parts of the night during the long Canadian winters. Work. Pub. Sleep. Repeat. And that's how he thought he would die and be remembered.

In his book *Unstoppable*, he recalls imagining his bio reading, "Craig had so much potential, and he spent all his time in the gym and at bars chasing girls. The rest of it he wasted..." Nobody would remember the years he spent grinding away to build his business. The ability to do whatever he wanted, whenever he wanted, didn't feel like freedom: it was breaking him.[1]

In and out of the emergency room in an hour, the doctors assured him that he was not having a heart attack, but a panic attack. The anxiety from long days and a lack of structure was crushing him.

He cleaned up his habits...for a few weeks. But without the momentum, progress, and daily wins from a structured life, he fell back into the old routine. Six weeks later, during a personal training session (where he was the trainer), he broke down again and asked *his client* to take *him* to the hospital.

After a battery of tests, the doctor came to the same conclusion: physically, he was fine. The racing heart and shallow breaths were symptoms of an anxiety attack. It was the lifestyle and coping mechanisms that were causing his physical symptoms. He was so spun up mentally, his body was revolting.

That was it.

He couldn't deny it anymore.

It was time he got his life together.

Craig studied, struggled, and began to structure his life in a way that eased his anxiety while making massive progress toward his goals. By setting non-negotiable ground rules, he created a system that allowed him true freedom. He was done with reactive mode, which led to action without accomplishment. That lack of accomplishment causes you to lose momentum.

In *Unstoppable*, Craig explains, "Without momentum, you lack motivation. No motivation, no action. No action, no progress. And the vicious cycle continues. The Antidote to a reactive, anxiety-ridden life is structure."[2]

That's exactly what happens to most people when they're working toward a goal. Work comes first, and then they make time for everything else. But that lack of structure and pushing away life outside of work leads to a spiral of putting out fires without making forward progress. Enter Craig's solution: the perfect week formula.

Ballantyne formed a structure that controlled his days, protected his personal time, and allowed him the freedom to make progress on his goals. That progress led to feelings of accomplishment and fulfillment. His anxiety slipped away as he gained positive momentum in his life.

The first step is to make a block of time every day that you hold sacred. Craig calls that "your magic time." He recommends placing this magic time first thing in the morning. During those early morning hours, your highest levels of focus and discipline are chauffeured by the least number of distractions. During your magic time you have one goal. It's the time reserved for your single most important task of the day. That is how you win your next hour and make progress on your goal.[3]

The rest of your calendar is designed to keep you productive, while not losing sight of the things that keep you motivated and energized. You block off time slots in your calendar to make sure you get the critical work done, but also have time for the *real* important things in life. The things that bring you joy and fulfillment, friends, family, self-care and hobbies.

Craig went from thinking he was having a heart attack in the hospital to coaching millionaires in the art of living. His anxiety was rooted in the chaos of attacking fires, and his freedom was found in building a life that cools off the coals before they ignite.

Turn Your Schedule Upside-Down

I was still a high school wrestling coach and PE teacher when we launched Caffeine and Kilos, a fitness lifestyle brand that sells coffee and apparel online. In hindsight, it makes sense how going from nonexistence to over one million dollars in the first calendar year caused some stress. But it was so new to us, we had no idea what was going on.

During the first year, my business partner Charlie was exhausted. A gym owner and fitness enthusiast, he couldn't understand why his skin burned, itched, and developed a rash all over. Begrudgingly, he went to a physician who immediately knew what was going on. He developed shingles from all the new stress in his life.

He was a good sport, so it was kind of funny to me. I remember joking with him, "What fit and healthy twenty-six-year-old gets shingles?"

About six months later, I noticed raised, red spots on my chest and neck. Following the advice of my wife, a nurse, I started taking allergy medication to keep the hives away. A few months went by and then it hit me, what fit and healthy twenty-nine-year-old has to take allergy medication to control stress hives? Turns out, the joke was on me.

I know lifestyle, not pharmaceutical intervention, should be the first line of defense against physical afflictions. I began looking for ways to control my stress. Meditating, breathing exercises, and books. After a few recommendations, I read Craig's first book, *The Perfect Day Formula.*

I blocked off my magic time and held it sacred. I began starting off every day by progressing on my most important task. I barreled through the rest of my day with a big win already under my belt. Winning my first hour of every day gave me the momentum to stack more wins throughout the day. And within weeks, I was able to cancel my Amazon subscription to Benadryl.

Over the last decade, I've modified Craig's plan to fit my life and combined it with other strategies that work for me. Here's how I structure my life to win my next hour and live the life I want: I block off certain times each day for the most important things in my life. The stuff that fills my cup and keeps me motivated. I'm home for family dinner at 5 p.m. every day. I get up early and complete my most important task during my magic time from 5:00 a.m. to 6:30 a.m. daily. I do some sort of exercise every day. The times in between are strategically filled with meetings and work blocks to attack my power list.

Here is how you can do it yourself. On Sunday, take thirty minutes to sit down and plan your week. Make a list of the most important things you need to get done to move your most important projects forward. Then, order that list from most important to least important. Now, put that list off to the side.

This is where the system turns most people's schedule upside down. Instead of falling into the trap of squeezing your life around your work, you're going to take the opposite approach.

Open your calendar and block off your magic time. Then, plug in what time you will dedicate to spending with your family or on personal relationships. Next you're going to fill in the things that keep you sane—exercise, self-care, and hobbies. For example, I know I'm going to CrossFit classes at Excel Health and Fitness every Monday and Friday at 8:30 a.m. and then a few other days at 6:30 a.m. depending on my wife's work schedule. I also find one or two days to go indoor rock climbing for thirty to sixty minutes.

Now that your magic time, family time, and personal time are blocked off, you can fill in work blocks. Plug in any meetings you have for the week and, in the gaps, you'll find work blocks. Make sure to group your meetings so your work blocks are around ninety minutes.

Go back to your to-do list for the week and turn your list into a schedule. The top items on the list are your most important tasks and need to be scheduled into your magic time. This is where your big goal becomes reality, where you focus and dominate your biggest undertakings. I'm using my magic time to write this book. Due to my investment and deadlines, it's the thing that absolutely must get done.

With the rest of the blocks, you have a choice. Craig Ballantyne, from earlier in this chapter, taught me his system. Go down your list and plug each item into your schedule where it best fits your days. In my hybrid system, I use those work blocks to knock out my power list. Every morning, I refer to my list and put the most urgent items into that day's power list.

Now you're ready for the week! As you go through your days, stick to your calendar. Every block of time is an opportunity to win your next hour. The system breaks down your weeks into days and days into blocks of time. You have less stress because although you have stuff to do, you already know when you're going to do it. No more hives, no more daily Benadryl. Just winning one hour after the next while turning your dreams into goals and goals into reality.

A 2011 study looked at happiness and freedom of time. Analyzing the results from over four hundred college students, the researchers found "that people who manage their free time well lead a better quality of life."[4] By blocking your days and structuring your free time you can truly experience freedom. You'll spend your days doing the things you really want to do, instead of stumbling through a life filled with stress and unfulfillment.

Measure Backward

Even with your weeks under control, there is one other spot where stress can pop up and discourage you. As you make progress and build the life you want, it's easy to look around at what others have already done and feel like you're not getting far enough or going fast enough. Getting down on yourself can lead to becoming unmotivated. John Powell famously stated, "Comparison is the death of true self-contentment."[5]

And that comparison creeps into your internal dialogue in different ways. The obvious one is comparing your progress to other people. But comparing yourself to where you want to be is just as dangerous.

Looking at how far you have to go can be discouraging. You need to focus on the gain instead of the gap.

In his book The Gap and the Gain, Dan Sullivan explains living in the gap "focuses on the gap between where you are now and where you want to be."6 By living in the gap, you only see the mountain ahead and the challenges awaiting you. Feelings of inadequacy can be overwhelming because you're not where you want to be.

Instead, measure yourself by looking at the gain, on how far you've come. This turns your focus to accomplishments and builds confidence. You already made it this far; you just need to keep going.

Looking back, you'll see a string of challenges you have already overcome.

Looking Back, Down the Mountain

Focusing on accomplishments rather than the long trail ahead is a lesson learned from building businesses and physical pursuits alike. It's a lesson I learned in the thin air of the Eastern Sierra Nevada mountains at twelve thousand feet in elevation. Eight hours into the hike, the sun finally quit playing peek-a-boo from behind the trees and decided to join us. The temperature would finally break above the freezing mark, which meant my neighbor Mike could finally drink water again after the hose from his camel back defrosted. We were almost to the shoulder of Mount Whitney, the highest peak in the forty-eight contiguous United States.

The funny thing is, I had no idea what I was getting myself into. Eight months prior, when Mike had asked if I wanted to climb Mount Whitney, I said, "Yeah, let's do it." I didn't really know what the project entailed, but I did know my father was once turned around just one mile from the top due to gusting wind that almost blew him off a cliff.

Two weeks before our departure date, Mike asked if I was ready. I again said, "Yeah, let's do it," and he asked what I was planning on wearing, because it would be seven degrees when we started hiking. That's when I realized I had no idea what I was getting into. Some people train for months or years to prepare for the altitude and strenuous trail. I wasn't worried about my physical conditioning, but now I was starting to worry about coming off the mountain with all ten fingers and toes.

We began the twenty-two-mile trek at midnight, relying on headlamps for light and trail mix for energy. The six thousand feet of elevation gain meant nearly every step was uphill the entire way. The trail mostly meanders through forest until you get above the tree line when the green foliage is replaced by gray granite. That's where things got serious.

The last stretch before traversing from the shoulder to the peak is where it happens. The section of trail referred to as "ninety-nine switchbacks" that climbs over 1,700 feet in just two miles. The prize for making it up all ninety-nine U-turns? Another full mile across the tops of granite pillars while wind forces you to crawl on all fours to avoid being blown off cliffs on the face of the peak.

One way to ensure being discouraged is to look ahead at how far you have to go. With the elevation nearing fourteen thousand feet, Mike and I would have to stop every third switchback to catch our breath. That makes thirty-three opportunities to look up toward the top and realize how far there is to go.

The only way we stayed motivated was to look back at how far we'd come. The benefit of being exposed on the side of the mountain is the clear view of the trail. We could look down to the switchbacks we'd already turned, down to the last alpine lake where we'd topped off our water, and down to the valley below where we began the trek.

Seeing how far we'd come was emboldening! We had already overcome three quarters of the trail and were making great progress. Measuring backward and celebrating our success kept us upbeat and drove us to keep putting one foot in front of the other. We only had to focus on our next turn of switchbacks, our next time block. We only had to win our next hour.

This takes us back to the "N" in the goal formula WIN. By noting the progress, you'll stay encouraged. Maybe you don't actually take out pen and paper on the hike, but even mentally noting your progress has a positive impact.

And at 10:30 a.m., we made it to the top. Being on the highest peak around, we could look down to the switchbacks we traversed and out as far as the eye can see. We weren't thinking about the eleven-mile hike back down to the car that would begin in the next thirty minutes. We were drinking in the success we had just secured while looking back at what we had done, and how far we had come.

People often use climbing a mountain as an analogy for starting a business or taking on a huge task. But we had literally made it to the top of the highest mountain in the lower forty-eight states. Focusing on the gain instead of the gap is what got us there.

Systems over Goals

Goals are great. They set the goalpost so you know what success looks like. They give you clarity on what you want to accomplish and by when. They give you a reason to celebrate success!

But goals by themselves need help to drive real progress. During our conversation, James Clear explained, "Goals are good for someone who wants to win once, but habits help you win over and over. When there's a gap between your goals and habits, your daily habits will always win."

Look at your goal, and think about what parts of your life you need to optimize to reach it. Ask yourself, What habits do I have that are holding me back? What habits do I need to be the type of person who accomplishes that goal?

If you have immediate clarity and self-awareness, fantastic. But most of us need a little help to identify our habits because most of them are part of our automatic operating system. You wake up, grab your phone, and sit on the toilet for thirty minutes doom scrolling social media. Without thinking about it, you just started your day by putting your brain in comparison mode. If your goal is to grow a business, that habit is holding you back.

The first step is discovering what your current habits are, and then figuring out what you need to change. Here's how you can get a vantage point of your life and habits:

1. Take a piece of paper and make a timesheet for your day in fifteen-minute blocks. Start it when you wake up and set the last time block for when you go to bed.
2. Starting when you wake up, set a timer to go off every fifteen minutes.
3. Write down exactly what you spent those fifteen minutes on every time the timer goes off.
4. Repeat for three days.

I know this process sounds cumbersome. It is. But it's necessary.

Within the first two hours of day one, you will have a few realizations about your life that you were previously oblivious to. At the beginning of day two, you'll start being aware of little actions you didn't notice before. And at the end of day three, you'll have a few things you know need to change to reach your goal.

Block off a full hour on day four to analyze your days at a deeper level. Which activities are not in alignment with your goal? Which blocks of time are you embarrassed about? What needs to change?

Now you have a glimpse into your current life. You can create the systems, which will turn to habits that serve you and lead to your goals. But how do you change habits that you perform without any prior thought?

Replace a new habit with the old by designing your environment to set you up for success. Remove friction to the new plan, and add friction to the old.

Here's what that can look like if you're the sit-on-the-toilet-while-your-legs-go-numb-first-thing-in-the-morning person. Take your phone off your nightstand before bed and put it in the kitchen. Use it as your alarm? No problem; stop doing that. Buy a cheap alarm clock and use that instead.

If you determined that reading business books will help you toward your goal, put a book on your nightstand where your phone used to sleep.

This little change will have multiple positive changes in your life. Habits often snowball together, making one positive change beget more positive changes. You may find that using an old school alarm also stops you from scrolling social media at night when you should be sleeping.

Even a small adjustment like charging your phone in the kitchen at night and putting a book on your nightstand can have incredible dividends toward growing a business. You'll start and end every day with a positive and productive habit instead of the one that doesn't serve you and your work toward the goal.

Win Your Next Hour

Before you go to bed tonight, get out three pieces of paper and a pen. Mark down fifteen-minute blocks for every hour you'll be awake tomorrow. Do it on all three sheets, to remove the friction of not following through on days two and three. Now put them next to the coffee pot so it'll be easy to begin tomorrow. Set that alarm for fifteen minute intervals, and learn about the daily habits you've been performing on autopilot.

CHAPTER 6

YOUR SUPERPOWER

Unfortunately, you don't have a choice. Skipping over the boring part doesn't work if you want to be successful. You have to slow down to speed up and master the basics before learning the complex. New skills are most efficiently attained by focusing on virtuosity.

Greg Glassman, founder of CrossFit fitness methodology, recalls how in gymnastics virtuosity is defined as "performing the common uncommonly well." He goes on to explain in his 2005 open letter titled *Fundamentals, Virtuosity, and Mastery*, "There is a compelling tendency among novices developing any skill or art, whether learning to play the violin, write poetry, or compete in gymnastics, to quickly move past the fundamentals and on to more elaborate, more sophisticated movements, skills, or techniques. What will inevitably doom... [progress] is a lack of commitment to fundamentals."[1]

A great example is in athletics. Nuances in footwork are often the difference between success and failure. The small details that are overlooked while watching the entire skill. We focus on the basketball going through the hoop, not on the stance the player was in when he released the ball or arm position when he caught the pass before shooting.

When I coached wrestling, Paul was one of my more... uh...interesting athletes. I don't think a comb passed through his hair in the four years I knew him. He also had a unique way of peeling an orange—hooking the rind on his bottom teeth before spinning the fruit, using his lower incisors like an apple peeler. And he wrestled without respect for tradition, rules, or conforming to any resemblance of established best practices. In his first year on the team, he ignored the small stuff, abhorred proven drills, and relied on one advanced move for all of his wins: the standing granby roll. All four of his wins out of thirty-two matches. Suffice it to say his unique style and individuality did not translate to desirable results.

He had convinced himself he could win because nobody was expecting "his move." And at the end of the season, he got knocked out of the league tournament in the first round because he never mastered the basics, and the other wrestlers were more skillful. But he loved wrestling and went to watch the state championship finals.

At the state finals, the fundamentals were what scored the most points. Double-leg shots for takedowns, half-nelsons for pins, and the stand-up to score from the bottom. At the highest level, it wasn't fancy techniques, but the expert execution of basics that won matches.

Paul left that night with an epiphany: the most common techniques in high school wrestling were effective against the best athletes if you perform the common, uncommonly well.

It was time for a change.

The next season, he came into practice with the goal of mastering the basics. When we drilled double-leg takedowns, he listened to the coaching staff and slowed down. Paul focused intently and made sure when he stepped forward on his drive step that he got his foot deep between the opponents feet. His head was on the outside hip providing pressure for when he turned the corner. He committed to doing all the small steps that would lead to success.

Paul's next wrestling season had a different ending. Instead of being knocked out in the second round, he earned a birth to the championship match! His first move in that match was a successful double-leg takedown, the first move a wrestler learns after a proper stance.

We see this lesson apply to every new skill, from athletics to art.

The street artist fnnch wasn't thinking of his work as a business when he got his first commission. During our conversation, he told me the origin story of how he began. He was illegally painting stencil pieces in public places for fun while focusing on improving the fundamentals of his practice, and someone took notice. That first commission led to another, which led to painting murals in a coffee shop, and soon after, placement in an art gallery. Most of his work is now produced in original multiples and sold directly to his fan base through his in-person shows and online sales. In 2023, he released a run of fifty-four original multiples every month for five hundred dollars, each and every month they sold out in minutes.

What separates fnnch from his contemporaries? He went from making illegal street art to commissioned murals all over the world, from stencil work.

How can stencil work stand out so much? It's in the details. Fnnch exemplifies virtuosity in his work.

Each piece is between seven and twenty layers. The colors are selected with precision before the stencils are laid and stacked. Minute details of every piece are precisely replicated. The common task of using a stencil we all learn in preschool has been practiced and refined to a level that is barely recognizable as the same skill.

If one layer is off by a sixteenth of an inch, the painting is ruined. If the layer isn't taped precisely, the paint will bleed, and the painting is ruined. If one pass of the aerosol can is too far away, too close, too heavy, or too light, the painting is ruined.

Fnnch is still improving on his techniques as he gains countless hours of practice, never settling on the quality of his work. He takes one part of the project and focuses on making it the best he can. He starts with designing the stencils. After illustrating the design, he breaks it down into layers. Then printing and cutting and testing are next. Each step getting the same attention as the previous one and taken in turn.

The entire project from start to finish takes many hours and is overwhelming. By focusing on his next hour, he takes the time to get it right.

Focusing on the details and performing the common, uncommonly well, will drive you toward success. It's easy to rush through the simple steps if you see a massive undertaking ahead of you. But when you focus only on winning your next hour, you'll give every step the attention it deserves. The only thing you have to do is this step to the absolute best of your ability.

If your goal is to lose weight and you are following a macros diet, you don't need a new fancy bathroom scale.

You need to hit your calories every day. If you want to start a business, you need to master the basics of sales. If you want to run across America, you need to focus on your running technique more than you need to wear seven computers on your body. If you want to open a coffee trailer, you need to make the perfect latte every order.

Virtuosity is your key to success. Drill the boring steps that build foundation to everything else. The basics are necessary before more complicated skills can be refined. The strength of your fundamental skills will determine the ceiling of your abilities. Without solidifying the basics, you'll never master advanced levels.

This is true for all complex skills, and few skills are more complicated than fixing a heavy barbell double your bodyweight overhead.

Coach Glenn Pendlay was a prolific coach in the sport of Olympic style weightlifting. In his book *The Glenn Pendlay Method*, author Seb Ostrowicz gives us a brief synopsis of his results. "He was the head United States coach at several international competitions. He produced over a hundred national champions from youth to senior level, as well as multiple Pan American Champions/ Games medalists."[2]

One of the reasons Coach Pendlay experienced prolific success was his obsession with details. Ostrowicz explained that as a competitive powerlifter in college, Pendlay "was noticed, and later approached by the legendary soviet head national weightlifting coach, Aleksey Medvedev." Being invited to Russia, Coach Pendlay took up the offer and went to Moscow for two weeks to learn from him.[3]

Following two weeks of intensive training, he left Moscow with two impactful lessons that shaped his coaching career:[4]

1. Positions are most important.
2. You should always do more repetitions.

After years of successful coaching, he was convinced to move from the state he loved, Texas, to California to coach a team of rising stars at California Strength.

Being an athlete on the California Strength team had a lot of perks. In a sport where there isn't much support, this team was loaded with opportunity. They paid for athletes' travel and entry fees to competitions. The training environment was the best imaginable with a room full of driven athletes pushing each other to attempts beyond their beliefs. And now the head coach was Glenn Pendlay. He was a living legend, with his name on barbells and bumper plates.

Training under Coach Pendlay was a transformative time for me as an athlete, coach, and person.

As an athlete on the team, the lessons I learned extended well beyond how to put the most weight overhead. At times I got little nuggets of advice while Coach was cooking the team lunch between training sessions. Other times, I learned from directives during training. Coach Pendlay was passionate about committing yourself fully to a pursuit. He believed training in a group to push one another is crucial and the path to success is through relentlessly pursuing excellence.

The most valuable lessons were peripherally picked up by watching him work with other athletes on the team. I replay one particular day in my mind every few months. It was ten years ago, but I can see it like I'm still in that training session now.

Out of the nine training sessions each week, Friday night was everybody's favorite. The session where Coach took the shackles off and let us fly. Max-out Fridays were a part of team culture where caffeine flowed, teammates shouted encouragement, and old personal records were demolished.

The building itself was sweating along with the team as condensation dripped down the painted cement walls. Two hours into training, we had built up to a maximum effort in all three lifts, followed by some additional technique and volume. Everyone was wrapping up their last training sets, except for one athlete Coach Pendlay was working with one on one.

Laurie was struggling in one lift: the jerk. The jerk is a very difficult movement that requires courage, timing, and precise footwork. The lift is accomplished by driving as much weight over your head as possible, with a heavy barbell starting on the front of your shoulders. Because the bar is too heavy to press overhead, you need to drop your body under it and catch it with arms locked out.

First, you bend your knees slightly to dip down, and then drive up as hard as you can to get upward momentum on the bar. As it leaves your shoulders, you push into it with your arms while dropping your body back down, under the bar. At the same time your arms lock out to fix the bar overhead, your feet need to land on the platform in a split stance—one leg in front of your body and one behind, similar to half-depth lunge. If your feet are too far apart, or not far apart enough, you'll fail and the bar will come crashing down to the ground (as you, hopefully, move out of the way).

It was Laurie's birthday, and she was crying. She could not get her front foot to cooperate and land with her heel under her knee. She would dip down, drive the bar, and then split her feet and land with her front foot three inches short of where it needed to be. Three inches may not sound like a lot, but when the barbell is heavier than your bodyweight half an inch is the difference between a make and a miss.

After a dozen failed attempts to fix her foot placement, Coach Pendlay had her break down the weight to less than fifty percent of her initial attempts to fix her technique. And she was still struggling.

"No, again," I remember him saying over and over again.

After three or four failed attempts, he would walk over and physically place her foot where it needed to be so she could feel it. Then it was up to her to replicate it during the lift.

Coach Pendlay corrected her, "No, farther out."

After a particularly poor attempt where her foot barely slid forward, he looked Laurie in the eyes and said the sentence that stands out the most after all these years: "That is the opposite of what we're trying to accomplish here."

The rest of the team had finished training thirty minutes prior and was waiting to go to team dinner for Laurie's birthday. But she was still working with Coach and struggling to get it right.

From an outsider's perspective, it would have appeared that Coach Pendlay was being cruel. Tears were running down Laurie's face on her birthday, while he stood there demanding excellence in this one little detail. But the lesson I learned that day is one that made a massive impact in my life.

As a coach, the worst thing you can do is tell someone something's right, when it's not. That would be cruel.

Ten years have passed, and Laurie has gotten married, changed positions at work, and moved from California to Tennessee. I haven't seen her in nearly a decade but wanted to know if she remembers that day, and whether she hates or loves Coach for it. So, I called her.

"I definitely remember him hammering me on a jerk drill. There were a few days like that," she recalled, chuckling. "But I never cried because I was upset with him. I was frustrated with myself. He held such a high standard; it pulled the best out of all of us. He was direct and matter of fact, but I knew it was coming from a place of help and a desire to see me achieve. I wanted to please him because I knew he wouldn't let me down and let me leave without getting the details right."

That day, Coach went over and calmed her down. He took a minute to re-assure her that she could and would get it. I'm not sure exactly what he said, but in her next four attempts she got it right every time. We were all cheering for her, shouting encouragement, and high fives were flying.

You're probably not a super awkward high school wrestler. It's unlikely you're a famous artist who started out with an outrageously illegal hobby. You may not be a weightlifter training to qualify for World Championships. So why does the most important skill for coaching people apply to you?

You are your own coach. Your own teammate. Your own artist.

Similar to when James Clear told me it's "better to ask, 'What can I stick to on my bad days?'" you should coach yourself to ask, "How can this detail be better?" Focus on making every detail one percent better every time, and after one hundred repetitions you'll be twice as proficient.

Let's look at what it took our favorite barista from chapter 1, Erica, to be successful with her coffee trailer.

First, the coffee had to be good. Yes, people loved how cute the trailer was—but if the coffee tasted like a burnt paper bag, nobody would care how Instagrammable the trailer was. She needed to be an expert at making coffee drinks. The first one definitely wouldn't be perfect, but they would be soon by focusing on each step to the best of her ability. The one hundredth latte she made was undoubtedly much better than the first one.

We can look at professional-snowboarder-turned-Tahoe-coffee-king, Nick Visconti. He explained to me that when he decided to hang up his signature boards, his first roast of coffee was...drinkable. But after volunteering at a local roaster for six months, he was able to open Drink Coffee Do Stuff, which now has three shops and is in major grocery stores all over northern California.

As a snowboarder, he missed way more tricks than he landed. It was often the tenth attempt when he actually landed the move. After each attempt, he made adjustments and improved. He took that lesson from snowboarding and applied it to roasting coffee and serving customers. Each detail gets its own focus, and the entire product gets better with each repetition.

This idea of virtuosity and practice is also something I've applied while learning to write and through the process of this book. A few years ago, I began writing a weekly newsletter because I had the gut feeling that writing was a skill that would help me be better at business. At the time, a coworker Mariel was running customer service for Caffeine and Kilos.

Mariel is an expert writer. Both of her parents are English professors, and she had ghost-written a handful of books for local fitness influencers and thought leaders. So, I did something that would make the high school version of myself cringe: I asked her to grade my papers. Through experience, I know the power of feedback and getting one percent better through focused repetitions on the basics.

I wrote my five-hundred-word article, then sent it to her for revisions. She would correct the spelling, grammar, punctuation, and help refine and reword the concepts. For nearly a year, she eviscerated my writing, and I went over each correction carefully. Each week, my article had fewer grammatical errors. Then fewer punctuation mistakes. Eventually, the corrections were focused on higher level concepts and storytelling.

As I'm writing this book now, I find myself talking to experts to get primary source quotes and information so I can bring more to the table than if I were regurgitating information you can read, watch, or listen to elsewhere. The first interview was rough. I found I was talking too much and trying to lead him to say what I wanted to write. Over time, I've gotten better at asking questions and then letting them explain. If I'm looking for unique quotes and ideas, I need to let them give me their thoughts, not mine. The interviews are much better, and the information has improved.

In business and life, people use a lot of sports analogies. This idea of focusing on the details until you perform the common uncommonly well is often referred to as "blocking and tackling." The most basic skills in football. When you start a business you need to sell, market, control costs, and dozens of other skills. But don't get so busy in the exciting, sexy stuff to overlook the basics. Focus on making the product great and the delivery a first-class experience. Focus on the basics, which are the foundation. Become an expert at blocking and tackling before you throw the long ball.

Win Your Next Hour

You can start now. Focus on improving one small detail in whatever you do next. If you are starting to run daily, start with putting on your shoes by making sure they are laced up perfectly—tight enough so you don't get blisters. Getting blisters will stop you from running tomorrow, or at least make it more uncomfortable and a dreaded task. So, you need to become an expert at tying your shoes. Next, focus on how your foot lands on the ground. What part of your foot strikes the ground first? Is it flopping down or pounding hard? Perfect the landing in each step. Keep working on the basics of every detail and watch your skills flourish. Now, go win your next hour one detail at a time.

CHAPTER 7

YOUR PEOPLE

You've heard them so much, they become meaningless soundbites.

> *"Your network is your net worth."*
>
> — TIM SANDERS[1]

> *"You are the average of the five people you spend the most time with."*
>
> — JIM ROHN[2]

> *"According to research by social psychologist Dr. David McClelland of Harvard, your reference group determines as much as 95 percent of your success or failure in life."*
>
> — DARREN HARDY[3]

You get it—the people in your life are important. But what does that mean when you're starting something new? What does that have to do with winning your next hour?

Learning to ask for help and the vulnerability to share your experiences are the biggest shortcuts to success.

Earlier, when breaking down our WIN acronym, we looked at "W" for words. Simply telling others what you plan to accomplish helps commit you to action through accountability and opens the door for others to help. But you can get so much further by actively seeking a person, or group of people, with shared experiences.

When Olympian Wes Kitts moved from Knoxville to California, he left a lot behind. During an interview, he broke down the timeline. He moved in January, went back home to get married in May, and his wife came to join him in June. Why would he do that? After all, he was training for the sport of weightlifting, and they definitely have barbells, weight plates, and squat racks in Knoxville.

Wes explained that with the goal of pursuing the Olympics, "there just wasn't much for me back home." California didn't have better barbells, but it had a better team, coach, and environment.

Moving to train at California Strength put him under the tutelage of Dave Spitz, a USA Weightlifting senior international coach who built an unmatched training environment. When people talk about California Strength, you hear the phrase, "There's something in the walls."

But the magic has nothing to do with the building. It has to do with the people's energy that has filled the room for over a decade, the opportunity to train alongside a team of people pursuing a similar goal. On days you don't feel like you're up to the rigors of hard training, it's a lot easier to put out when you're sharing the experience with others. You can borrow the energy from your teammates' successes.

When you're approaching the bar alone without any eyes on you, it's easy to make an excuse. But when your teammates and coach are watching, you feel an obligation to give your absolute best. You learn from other people's mistakes and get inspired by their wins. As a member of the California Strength weightlifting team, I personally experienced the power of environment.

I had just competed in my third weightlifting meet and decided the sport was something I would pursue. After hearing about a clinic just an hour away coached by the legendary Glenn Pendlay, I signed up to learn how to be a better lifter. The clinic changed my lifting, but not how I expected. What I learned about technique paled in comparison to what I learned about environment.

Assisting Coach Pendlay were members of the team, two of whom had just earned gold medals at National Championships. Watching them motivate people with their words and actions during the clinic made it clear that was the place I needed to be to fulfill my potential.

Training under one of their star athletes, Jon North, I learned how hard I needed to work. When I was eventually invited to join the team and train under Coach

Pendlay, I learned much more. Matching weight plates so both sides of the bar are the same brand, a clean floor, and the perfect cues don't matter. Shouts of encouragement, watching people succeed, and lifting up people when they fail do.

Pendlay believed in the training environment. In his book *The Glenn Pendlay Method*, Seb Ostowicz recalls how Coach "strove to create an environment of competition every single session, regularly encouraging multiple maximum effort lifts from athletes to beat their teammates."[4] Coach Pendlay explained in his blog *Dynamis*, "Getting two or three lifters together who are lifting similar numbers in the same weight class always leads to improved results... no one likes to lose."[5]

After three years on the team, I tore my rotator cuff and had to take the side lines for a few months to undergo surgery. Coming off a shoulder injury, my training was modified. I could do heavy cleans but wasn't yet able to jerk the maximum effort weights overhead.

When I showed up on Friday night, Big Mike looked at me and asked, "Well, since you're just doing the clean, are you going to hit one hundred and seventy-five kilos tonight?"

At that point, my best lift was one hundred and seventy-three kilos. I looked him in the eye and brazenly replied, "I might mess around and hit one hundred and eighty."

It was a cold night in January. The body heat from twenty people pushing their physical limits created a fog in the room that condensed and trickled down the painted cement walls. The music was so loud you could only hear weights slamming against the ground, coach yelling "more" after made lifts, and athletes coercing their legs to wake up and push harder by slapping themselves on the thighs before big attempts.

Mike didn't scoff or laugh. He took a step closer and said, "If you clean one-eighty, I will give you one hundred dollars...wait." He reached in his bag and pulled out a one-hundred-dollar bill and placed it on the ground in front of my platform with a weight covering one corner so it wouldn't blow away. That put me in the zone!

Sharing a bar with Big Mike, we built up—one-forty, one-fifty, one-sixty, one-sixty-eight, one-seventy-five.

If I was training alone, I would have stopped. I had just hit a lifetime personal record! You see, the thing about hitting a PR is it comes along with an adrenaline dump. Sometimes training for a full year will only yield a two- or three-kilogram PR. It's always cause for celebration! But because I was there with the team, with Big Mike betting against me, I wasn't done.

Big Mike told me to sit down and loaded the barbell for me. One hundred and eighty kilos were on the platform with the one-hundred-dollar bill pinned to the ground in front of it. And that's when Big Mike changed his tune. Instead of telling me I was crazy, he began to root for me. The entire gym stopped, watched, and screamed taunts of motivation. I stepped up the bar and pulled on it.

Getting the weight up to my hips, I drove hard through the ground, changed directions, and pulled myself under the bar meeting it with the front of my shoulders as I found the bottom of my squat. As I went to stand up, the bar forced me back down. Catching the bounce in the bottom a second time, I drove harder seeing only the fog in the room and hearing only the shouts of my team.

I stood up with the bar on my shoulders, looked at Big Mike, and slam the bar down. He was ecstatic! I've never seen someone so happy to lose a bet. And that's the point—he put the money down to motivate me. He knew coming back from shoulder surgery is more mentally challenging that it is physically. Without my team, my coach, and my people, I would have never attempted that weight.

That's the environment Wes Kitts left his hometown to be a part of. Training alone in Tennessee he would never have been pushed that way. He wouldn't have a coach with the experience of Dave Spitz to learn from and collapse time. On a cold Friday night in January, without the encouragement of training partners, he would probably wrap up training early, content with hitting acceptable numbers and rushing home to snuggle on the couch with his fiancée.

The environment of the team is the perfect example of two types of people you need when you're turning your dreams into goals, and goals into reality. A coach who has been there before and peers who are alongside you on the same journey. Being around other athletes pursuing big dreams has a dramatic effect on your goals and what you think is possible. Being around those pursuing the same goal as yourself is reassuring and motivating. If you can, what's better is to be around those who are chasing bigger dreams than yourself. That was the power of the California Strength weightlifting team.

My goals in weightlifting were to stand on the podium at National Championships. But my teammates had their sights on the Olympic podium. Training there changed my frame of mind about what was possible.

When I started training there, I wanted to qualify for a national-level meet. I was training alongside two teammates who were National Champions. Of course I could qualify; these guys had won! And they set me out on a journey I would have never penciled for myself. In March, I was told, "This year you're going to qualify for the American open, then next year qualify for National Championships. You'll place top ten at the American Open, then begin winning medals at Nationals."

They laid the expectations for me to win medals at the national level within the next two years, a timeframe I hadn't imagined was possible. Their belief in me, paired with the proof of their own results, made me believe in the plan. Over the next two years, I placed seventh at National Championships and fifth at the American Open. Both places were far beyond what I had ever set my eyes on before they showed me what was possible. Taking those lessons with me led to winning gold at Masters World Cup seven years later.

Maybe you're not pursuing athletics. Maybe there isn't necessarily a team you can join to help you with your goal of growing your business or losing weight or whatever else you're after. Here's the good news: those two sets of people are available in every pursuit in life. Striving to be around others who have shared experiences is how I met Angela who introduced me to the publisher I'm using for writing this book.

It began when I got coffee with a friend who was in town for the week, and he kept talking about this group of business owners that were helping each other out. I knew Gabe as a gym owner, but a few years back he shut down his gym and moved his family to Nashville. While in Nashville, he met someone, and they started a window washing company. Gabe being a master at sales, they began to take over Broadway Street and soon were washing the windows of every major bar in town.

Wanting to know more about home service businesses, he and his partner reached out to some other local business owners. They would get together every quarter and share. They shared their struggles along with their big wins. Each person presented an idea that worked for them to make ten thousand dollars, and that others could implement within the next quarter. They discussed hiring problems, employees they suspected were stealing, and what marketing was working.

Each quarter, everyone was growing, adapting, and becoming more successful. Over the course of eighteen months, the group went from four people to twenty-four.

At that coffee shop in California, Gabe invited me to go check it out. He pitched me, "I know you're not in home services, but business is business. You have employees. You do marketing. You're trying to reduce costs. Come out next month and check it out. We feed you breakfast and lunch, and at the end of the day you get to hang out at a private club to drink bourbon and smoke cigars."

Of course I was in!

As the one guy who wasn't in home services, I ended up learning a ton. Coming home, I had plans for my gym, Excel Health and Fitness, and clarity on goals for my e-commerce company, Caffeine and Kilos. I soon realized more important than the specific takeaways were the relationships I had developed.

These relationships became shortcuts to success. I met Dave, an expert in Google search engine optimization, and implemented his strategies. When I have a question, I can call him. When I was approached with an investment opportunity in another company, I asked Mike who runs a capital firm that specializes in small business investments, turnarounds, and growth. Needing help with a phone answering service, I talked to Brant, the owner of an incoming call center.

And when Angela walked in with a heavy box full of copies of her new book, I asked her how she went about writing it and getting it published.

Taking the risk of flying to Nashville for a single day of meeting with other business owners has resulted in better business practices and unique opportunities. These included hiring practices, leadership skills, writing this book, multiple investments in other companies, experts who are a text message away, an ice fishing trip to Minnesota, and friends who are there when I'm struggling and need to call someone who can relate. Instead of focusing on my to-do list, I decided to win my next hour and meet with Gabe. When he invited me to go check out the group, I took action and booked my flights instead of waiting to decide if it would be worth my time.

Waiting for your version of Gabe to invite you to coffee and hopefully to his group may not be the best way to find your tribe. You don't have to wait and wish. Take action and create a group environment yourself. If you don't have any friends that can help, go make some.

If you own a coffee shop, go to the next town over and visit their shop. Ask for the owner and introduce yourself. Get to know them a bit, and make sure to do the most important thing: be vulnerable. Share with them what is working for you and what's not. Tell them your struggles and successes, biggest mistakes, and epiphanies. Find a way to help them.

Do you have a nearby business you can collaborate with? Maybe you know a florist whose flowers you can feature in your shop? Or a hairdresser whose clients you can serve free coffee to one morning. The next week, repeat with another shop. Some people may not be open or see the value in it, but some will. Over the course of just a few months, you'll have made some friends in the industry who are open to sharing and growing together.

Look outside your direct industry. What businesses are next to yours? Go make friends with the owners. You'll find many similarities in your struggles, despite being in different industries. You'll also find ways to work together on promotions that benefit both companies. Another route is to join the local Chamber of Commerce.

After attending the Nashville group for a year, I realized how much I needed something similar but directly related to e-commerce. Over the last ten years selling coffee and apparel in the fitness space, I know many business owners who are running similar companies. It was time to reach out and get the gang together.

Too often people who run businesses are hesitant to talk to other business owners in the same market and industry out of fear of competition. They think people might steal their ideas or have some unfair advantage if they are vulnerable enough to share their struggles. I've found the exact opposite while running small businesses.

Successful business owners have a growth mindset, not a scarcity mindset. Their goal isn't to make their share of the pie bigger, but to grow the whole pie. They believe plenty of customers and money are available, and their business can thrive by pursuing excellence, not by damaging others.

I reached out to Andy, Ryan, and Jason. All three own and operate e-commerce companies that sell apparel. Two of them are directly in the fitness space, just as Caffeine and Kilos is. They were all stoked to get together and share.

Booking a house in Reno for two nights, we spent the morning hiking to the top of the nearest hill and the day talking about what's working and what's not working in our businesses. In the second morning, we all left and went back to our companies with clarity, ideas, and a closer friendship that can be called upon when we need help.

The power of groups goes far beyond business networking and athletic teams. Maybe your goal is to be a better father, mother, husband, or brother. As we get older, we lose the built in friendships of classrooms and the playground.

My friend Wes Piatt had been out of the military for six years. He's competed for title of Fittest on Earth at the CrossFit Games, owns his own gym, and has a beautiful family with his wife, two daughters, and a labrador retriever.

But he knew something was missing as he found himself battling depression. He desperately wanted to be a better man. A better husband, father, and mentor in his community. He felt like he was falling short in all three aspects and didn't know where to get help. Combine that helplessness with PTSD from the Iraq War and the 2020 COVID-19 crisis, and Wes was in trouble. He felt pushed to the brink of contemplating suicide.

As one last effort, he made a simple post on social media. He was looking for other men, other dads who want to help each other out to be better fathers and husbands.

The response was twenty guys replying that they also had the desire to better themselves. I was one of the twenty.

I've read a few books on parenting and spousing. I knew this would be different through my experiences with the power of peers in sports and business. Learning from the shared experiences of others who are living similar lives is the best way to improve.

Wes set up the group on a group video messaging platform, and a community was born. Dads from Wisconsin, California, Washington, Texas, and North Dakota started asking for and sharing advice. Over the next year, we helped each other with the way we talked to our daughters, the way we showed our wives love, and the way we backed into parking spaces.

Men in the group went through divorces and others saved their marriages. Some moved to different states and others bought a home near their parents. Everyone focused on winning their next hour and improving the world around them.

Wes found what he was missing: a group of guys where he could ask for help and share his wins. He found a community that helped each other through tough times and celebrated victories together. He formed a community. (If you're looking for a group to help you through the rigors of being a father and husband, check out Webus on Instagram @webusint.)

Turning to groups for support, comfort, and honesty isn't new. Alcoholics Anonymous was established in 1935 and has helped more than two million alcoholics stop drinking. The program is centered around a twelve-step process that includes attending meetings a minimum of once a week for six months or more.

The website for American Addiction Centers cites a story published in the Journal of Addictive Disease that "showed abstinence rates of those recovering from alcohol abuse at one year and 18 months. Approximately, 20-25% of those who didn't attend a 12-step program, such as AA, or another aftercare program were abstinent from alcohol and drugs after one year. On the other hand, the abstinence rate was nearly twice as high for those who attended AA or another similar 12-step program without any aftercare. The results were evident that the more meetings people attended, the greater the chances of alcohol and drug abstinence."[6]

Many experts believe attending the meetings is the most beneficial part of the entire twelve-step program. The program Practical Recovery explains, "In such a group, participants can describe their own experiences and express their feelings about them, identify individuals (models) to emulate, realize that however much they have struggled, others may have struggled even more, discover alternative solutions for problems they have faced, learn about problems that might occur in the future and ways to solve them, experience the care and concern of others, and momentarily transcend their problems by caring for others."[7]

You don't have to pursue your goals alone! It's inefficient to do so. Every mistake you make will cost you time, energy, money, and motivation. That is not to discourage you; mistakes are an inevitable part of every journey that turns dreams into goals and goals in reality. You cannot be afraid to make mistakes. But why make more mistakes than necessary?

By talking to others who have done what you're doing, or are doing it concurrently, you can learn from their mistakes and avoid them yourself. It's like swapping out diesel gasoline for rocket fuel.

Another way to learn from others and minimize mistakes is to hire a coach. If your goal is to lose weight you can hire a personal trainer. If your goal is to start a business, hire a business coach.

In chapter 5, we met Craig Ballantyne, a small business owner whose anxiety was killing him until he created a system and schedule for himself: the perfect week formula. After overcoming his anxiety, Craig Ballantyne's business took off. He has since used his story and lessons to help thousands of entrepreneurs grow their businesses by overcoming their fears and failures. In his book Unstoppable, Craig explained his benefits when hiring his first coach: "Coach gave me outside eyes, a blueprint, a step-by-step guide for success, and most importantly, the no-holds barred accountability."[8]

During a coaching session in San Diego with Craig, he detailed how hiring a coach is a way to compress time. The coach has already been down the road and can guide you to avoid costly mistakes, as well as highlight the most beneficial path forward. They rely on their own experiences, as well as the experiences of everyone else they've coached. All that knowledge can be applied to your journey, helping you go further and faster than if you stumbled your way through alone.

If you can find a coaching program where you meet with a coach and a group of your peers, you multiply the benefits of both. You can relate to your peers and learn what is currently working and not working from them. You also grow your network and have people you can collaborate with. And it's all done under the guidance of a coach who can help guide which ideas to pursue and which to avoid.

Whenever you're stuck, the answer is always people.

Win Your Next Hour

Be open to meeting with people and discussing your goals. Make a list of people to reach out to who are pursuing a similar goal as you. Look for a group to join that can help support you and give you the accountability you need. And finally, look up a few coaches to see who resonate with you and can help you level up.

CHAPTER 8

YOUR GOAL-SETTING PLAN

Now it's time to take action and set goals. This process shouldn't take that long; my clients complete it from start to finish in a ninety-minute workshop I coach. Since you've already learned many of the frameworks involved, it'll be a breeze. You're going to exit this chapter with clarity on your goal and a plan of action in just six simple steps.

You'll determine what you really want by acting like a four-year-old. Then, you'll set a date for completion. We'll review process goals and how habits will shape our results. You'll learn what character traits are important for your goal and become accountable to yourself and others. A series of worksheets will help you, and you can get them all for free at dannylehr.com/worksheets.

Step 1: Your Five WHYs

To get clarity, you need to know exactly what you want and why you want it. As you progress down your chosen path, you'll come across many challenges. The way to continue and fight for your dream is to know the true why behind your pursuit.

Why do you want to lose eighty pounds?
Why do you want to open a gym?
Why do you want to go to grad school?

To find out your true why, you need to act like a four-year-old. It's time to complete the "5 WHY's Worksheet." Grab your worksheet, or a pen and paper, and write it out. If you're creating your own worksheet, title it "Clarity Is Key," and then create seven sections below the title.

Clarity is Key
My Goal (?)

The "5 Why's" of Clarity...

Why?

Why?

Why?

Why?

Why?

In the first section, write your goal. What is it that you think you want to accomplish? For this exercise, we'll use the example of someone who wants to lose eighty pounds. You would write in the top section: "My goal is to lose eighty pounds."

Now it's toddler time. You're going to ask yourself every toddler's favorite question: *why*? After answering in the next section down, harness your inner toddler and ask *why* about your answer until you've filled in the middle five sections. Continue until you've asked and answered why five times. Don't quit early; get all five answers down.

Label the last section, "My Real Goal."

In that section, you're going to write the answer to your fifth *why* or an epiphany you came across that got to the root of your desire.

Here's how it could play out in our example:

Goal: I want to lose eighty pounds.

Why? I'm out of breath when I walk more than fifty feet.

Why? I'm out of breath because I'm carrying around all this extra weight and I don't exercise.

Why? I don't exercise because I don't have the energy.

Why? I don't have the energy because I don't eat healthy foods.

Why? I don't eat healthy foods because I lack discipline and don't respect myself.

My Real Goal: I want to treat my body with respect.

When you get your *real goal*, it's a peek behind the curtain of the driving force behind your dream. Occasionally, you may want to re-work your goal based on a realization. Most often your dream stays the same, but your clarity and motivation become stronger.

Now that you have completed your internal deep dive and understand your true *why*, we can move forward and set you up for success.

Step 2: Date of Completion

When do you want to have completed your goal by? If you're not sure of an exact date, don't overthink it. Just pick one. You have to have one because dates and deadlines are what differentiate a dream from a goal.

If you don't know exactly how long it will take, that's okay. You can always adjust. Over the course of completing this goal-setting plan, you may have some "a-ha" moments and come back to recalibrate your date of completion.

Step 3: Understanding Process Goals (You Are What You Do)

In chapter 5, we learned to focus on habits and systems in your day-to-day. If your goal is big, the date of completion may be months or years away. It's easy to lose motivation when the deadline is far into the future. In the meantime, focus on your daily habits and process goals.

Process goals are checkmarks along the way to make sure you're on track to turn your dream into your reality. It's a road map you can follow to stay on track. Process goals can come from two categories: checkpoints and habits.

Checkpoints are crucial to make sure you're following the right path and making progress in the right direction. If you're going to take a road trip across the country, you first need to determine what route you're going to take—which highways you will travel, which states you will drive through, and where you plan to sleep on the journey. Who knows where you'd end up if you got in your car and started driving without charting your course.

As you think about your goal, small accomplishments are along the way. We've all heard the trite expression to "enjoy the process." Part of that is celebrating the small wins along the way to stay encouraged.

Your habits are another form of process goals. What habits do you need to create that will lead you toward your goal? What's great about creating these habits is they make progress seem like a side-benefit. It becomes something that just happens without big efforts and daily motivation. Discipline will help you get the habits rolling, then they will carry you when motivation is hiding under the covers.

When I decided to write this book, I knew it was a big undertaking. The time to plan the outline, write the rough draft, edit for content and context, clean it up at a sentence level, and market it along the way is overwhelming. I had so much to do and a timeline that must be followed.

First, I charted a course by signing up for program with a publisher that would hold me accountable. Meeting every week with a series of editors, I had to get the work complete or I'd be on a Zoom call explaining to someone why I didn't do what I had committed to. The journey was laid out in front of me. In six weeks, the outline will be ready, in four months the rough draft will be complete, and in eight months the book will launch. I knew what direction I was headed and had checkpoints along the way.

Next, I needed to use discipline to create habits that keep me on track on days I didn't "feel like" getting the work done. My habit was simple: every morning after brewing up some Caffeine and Kilos coffee, I sat down in my writing chair with my laptop and worked on the book. Monday, Tuesday, and Wednesday, I wrote eight hundred words. Thursday, I met with my editor. Friday, Saturday, and Sunday, I conducted interviews and worked on revisions.

Many nights, my sick kids woke me up throughout the night followed by 4:45 a.m. alarms that entered my dreams before rousing me. There were early morning trips to the airport that I didn't leave for until I was out of my writing chair. One morning, I told the flu it had to wait until I finished my interview before it could steal the rest of my day.

It didn't matter how I felt. What mattered was putting down eight hundred words at a time and finishing the book. That daily habit of morning work carried me through valleys of discipline and motivation. Every day was a day I made progress, and every eight hundred words I got on the page was a small victory.

Find your process goals that will provide you opportunities to celebrate and habits to keep you on track.

There is a worksheet in your download packet to help with your process goals. If you don't have access, you can flip your "5 WHY's" sheet over and complete this on the back.

My Process Goals

Process Goals: In order to reach my goals, I am going to ...

24 Hours:

____

48 Hours:

____

7 Days:

____

Date: _______________

My Goal

By _______ , I will have

____

My reason for this is

____

____

____

____

Signed: _______________

At the top, write today's date. It may seem unnecessary, but do it anyway.

Create a section titled "My Goal," followed by the sentence: By __________, I will have _____________________.

You don't have to leave the blanks, so go ahead and fill those in.

The next line is as follows: My reason for this is _______________________________.

In that blank is where you fill in your true reason discovered by your 5 WHY's.

On the side, or under your *why* complete the following:

In order to reach my goals, I am going to:

In twenty-four hours: _______________

In forty-eight hours: _____________________

In seven days: ___________________

Daily focus: ____________________

At the very bottom middle of the page, write:

Signed _______________________________

Don't sign the bottom yet; put this sheet off to the side and we'll finish up shortly.

Step 4: Visualize Future You

Ah, Future You. The person who you can be kind to or set up for absolute failure and misery. I sometimes joke about "Future Danny." When I was competing in weightlifting, I hyperextended my elbow a few times. National championships were just a few months away, and I knew I'd be competing. I made the choice to train on an injured arm before it was healed, knowing I was exacerbating the problem and causing damage that would need to be dealt with a few years down the road. But that was Future Danny's problem. It's also why I had the elbow surgery that hindered my progress on this book for a few days.

Plugging in your phone on the other side of the room (or in a different room) to stop in-bed-doom-scrolling and going to sleep at a reasonable time is being kind to Future You. Choosing to not eat that fourth...and fifth piece of pizza because you know how it will make you feel in an hour is being kind to Future You.

But we often make choices knowing we'll pay for them later. That *one more* glass of wine, even though you should be going to bed? That's Future You's problem. Buying that car you really want even though the payments will put a major strain on your finances? A problem for Future You.

We usually know we'll regret it down the road, but give in to our impulses now. One way to navigate around these pitfalls is to make yourself *feel* the future. Instead of focusing on the external ramifications, focus on how you'll *feel* when the ramifications hit. Be nice to Future You!

Now let's visualize how your life will be when you do follow through on your plans. Close your eyes and picture your future when you're celebrating accomplishing your goal.

What is the date? What exactly are you celebrating? If your goal is to open a coffee trailer, maybe you're at the grand opening. Or maybe you're celebrating selling your hundredth cup of coffee.

Now that you know the when and the what, it's time to focus on people. Who's with you? A theme that runs through nearly every section of Win Your Next Hour is people. Think of who you want to be there with you. It might be friends, family, or even a mentor or connection that you haven't made yet but will help you get to the next level.

We'll shift now to looking internally. The next few lines are a peek into the type of person you need to become to take that step. Crushing your goals will require you to change. As scary as that may sound, think of it as exciting! Don't push back by thinking that you, exactly how you currently are, can accomplish your goal. If that was true, you would have already done it.

It may help to brainstorm using our ten ideas framework from chapter 2. Make a list of ten activities or character traits of someone who has already accomplished your goal. What are ten things they do? Then, make another list of ten things they do not do. If your goal is to lose forty pounds, how does someone who lost forty pounds behave? Do they sit on the couch and demolish a pint of ice cream three nights a week? What do they order when they go out to dinner? How often do they hit the snooze button instead of going to the gym in the morning?

What are the habits and activities you need to start, or stop, to reach your goal? Now fill in the next three lines: "Now I...," "I also...," "I never...."

The last line is "I feel..." That one will make you smile. If it doesn't, you should probably change your goal.

At that moment of celebration, how do you feel? You're at the event surrounded by the people who you want to be there, reflecting on your new life. How does that feel? You need to remember that feeling. When your journey gets tough, come back to it. Remember what it's going to feel like when you accomplish your goal! Let that feeling drive you when you're challenged.

It's important to think about your feelings because your thoughts change your physiology. An article in the National Library of Medicine titled "Physiology, Stress Reaction" explains:

"A stressful situation, whether environmental or psychological, can activate a cascade of stress hormones that produce physiological changes. Activation of the sympathetic nervous system in this manner triggers an acute stress response called the "fight or flight" response. This enables a person to either fight the threat or flee the situation. The rush of adrenaline and noradrenaline secreted from the adrenal medulla causes almost all portions of the sympathetic system to discharge simultaneously as a widespread mass discharge effect throughout the entire body. Physiologic changes of this mass discharge effect include increased arterial pressure, more blood flow to active muscles and less blood flow to organs not needed for rapid motor activity, increased rate of blood coagulation, increased rates of cellular metabolism through the body, increased muscle strength, increased mental activity, increased blood glucose concentration, and increased glycolysis in the liver/muscle. The net effect of all these effects allows a person to perform more strenuous activity than normal. After the perceived threat disappears, the body returns to pre-arousal levels."[1]

Psychological stress can change the way our body reacts. We can look at a few ways many of us have experienced this in our lives.

The increased heart rate before getting on a roller coaster. The adrenaline dump when you nearly avoid a car accident, causing you to shake. The "physical changes" in your pants when thinking about some alone time with your spouse. These are all physical changes in your body created in your mind.

Also consider how your thoughts can lead to emotions and physical changes that drive forward more of the same thoughts.

You have that one coworker. You know, the one always in a bad mood who makes you feel on edge around him. On the drive to work, you find yourself thinking about how he wronged you last week. You just *know* he's going to say something today that'll piss you off. Next thing you know, you're having an imaginary argument with him during your drive. Your heart rate increases and your face reddens with that *I wish he would* anger.

You walk into work, and he is there working at his desk.

He turns and says, "Good morning."

You cringe and reply, "Go suck an egg."

Visualizing the future you want and letting yourself experience the emotions that will accompany your success will help shape your thoughts. The emotions that contribute to your success can replace the fear that guides poor choices.

You Can
See It

Your Vision

The date is:

____

What are you celebrating?

- -

Who is there?

- -

I also

- -

Now I

- -

I never

- -

I feel

- -

Don't skip this step. You must realize who you are going to become by accomplishing your goals! Grab your worksheet titled "You Can See It." If you don't have the worksheet, fill out a blank sheet with the following outline:

The date is: _____________

What are you celebrating? _______________

Who is there? ____________________________

Now I ______________________________________

I also ____

I never ____

I feel ____

Step 5: Your Goals Sheet with Signature

Now it's time to pull out your goals sheet and double-check it. Now that you've seen the Future You who will accomplish your goal, do you think anything needs to change? Look over your process goals you'll complete in twenty-four hours, forty-eight hours, and seven days. Are they still where you want to start?

Make any necessary changes, then fill in the next line, Daily Focus. What is a daily habit you can accomplish every day that will help you become the Future You who accomplishes your goal?

It's time to commit to your vision. Sign the page. You are creating a contract with yourself to follow through on the steps you've outlined.

It may seem a little silly to sign an agreement with yourself, but signing a contract at the beginning makes a huge difference. An article published in Proceedings of the National Academy of Sciences (PNAS) found "[i]n a series of studies looking at honesty in reporting... participants were less likely to lie when they signed a commitment to be honest before... The act of signing brought thoughts of ethics into their minds, serving as a reminder of their desire to be honorable." In fact, "the simple act of signing their names to commit to honesty at the beginning."[2]

So, commit to yourself now, at the beginning, to dramatically increase your commitment and follow through.

Step 6: Accountability

I learned parts of this workshop from Craig Ballantyne, the business coach who went from anxiety-riddled hospital trips to coaching billionaires. Craig teaches "accountability is the secret sauce. And the special ingredient in the special sauce is to be accountable to someone you deeply do not want to disappoint."

If you have hired a coach, that person works great. One of the biggest perks of hiring a coach is there's somebody you meet with regularly who will hold you accountable to the things you said you were going to do. It's why I took piano lessons when I was thirty-four years old.

My oldest daughter Maddie was four years old and wanted to start piano lessons. My father played the trumpet in band as a student and in church as an adult. That encouraged my brother and I to play instruments, and my brother Brian used his full-ride scholastic scholarship to earn a bachelor's degree in music. Through that upbringing, I saw the value in music from a young age. So, I signed Maddie up with a local piano instructor.

I had wanted to take lessons for a few years myself, but I was busy collecting excuses for why it was always a bad time to start—the kids, business, coaching, etc. However, now that I was taking my daughter every week to the lessons, I was already there. The thirty-minute lessons would just be thirty minutes out of my day. I brought a book or laptop to use during Maddie's lesson and she brought coloring books or toys to entertain herself during mine.

But why did I need to take lessons? I know how a piano works, and I know how to read music. By starting with the beginner-level books, I could surely teach myself through the first few levels.

But I never did.

I had thought about it many times, but it never seemed like a good time to practice. I had no accountability, so learning and practicing piano was always pushed down the priority list, tucked under more important things like learning to make craft cocktails, sitting outside on nice days, and every other thing I've ever done.

The only way I would start is with the help of accountability. Once I started taking lessons, I practiced every day. Practicing piano for just twenty minutes moved up the priority list and claimed a spot right under eating food and drinking water.

I was paying for the lessons, but the dollar value wasn't high enough to be a huge motivator. Yes, I really enjoy playing music, but I also enjoy cocktails outside on nice days. What moved learning piano up the priority ladder was the accountability. The thought of sitting down in front of my instructor having made zero progress from the week before was terrifying. If it was obvious I wasn't practicing and improving between lessons, I would be embarrassed. It would be showing up to tell someone I didn't do what I said I would and was wasting both our time.

If you don't have a coach you can meet with regularly, public accountability is a great way to go. Business coach and entrepreneur Craig Ballantyne used public accountability to stop cursing. One day he posted to all his social media that he would no longer be using swear words. From that day forward, if he let one slip publicly, he would feel like a fraud and he knew others would call him out.

Once I started posting about writing this book, people started asking me about it. I could not turn back without conversations about me not following through on something I had publicly committed to.

A little trick also works if you don't care about anyone: the cat food diet.

The cat food diet is a way to drive commitment and create a scenario where the consequence sounds so appalling, following through becomes the easy choice. The best part is the simplicity. If you don't follow through on your plan, you have to eat a can of cat food. Talk about motivation!

If that seems ridiculous, good! That's why it works. You can always swap out eating a can of cat food for something else that fills that same roll. The goal is to find something that will push you to follow through.

Another self-motivation technique is a financial punishment. If you don't follow through, you have to donate a sum of money to a charity that you do not agree with. Pick one that goes against your political beliefs; maybe it's even a political donation to the leading candidate from the opposing party.

The key is to find a consequence that makes your stomach churn when you simply consider the possibility.

Win Your Next Hour

Take an hour and complete all the exercises in this chapter. You can get them all done in that time, and you'll have complete clarity on your next move.

DO IT LIKE THIS

It's time for action.

After completing the goal setting sheets from chapter 8, you know what you want, why you want it, and you have a roadmap to get started. But there's a critical step you need to be cautious of: Procrastination by fury.

You must avoid taking action and being busy on tasks that don't actually move you forward, like stomping on the gas pedal of a truck stuck in the mud.

The engine roars while the tires throw mud, but the truck doesn't *go* anywhere.

All that energy expended without any forward progress. If that's how you start your project, you'll be invigorated at first, then quickly become frustrated and tired before creating any momentum. That frustration will dishearten, and your new business will flounder as you quit on your dream.

If you take action on the steps that drive you forward, that frustration won't be your experience. Working on the critical tasks will drive progress, and you'll be energized as each little success will be motivation and encouragement to continue.

Noah Kagan grew up in the northern California Bay Area surrounded by startups and new technology companies. Staying local and attending University of California, Berkley, he always planned to work for the next big thing when he finished school. At twenty-four years old, he was hired as employee number thirty at an up-and-coming company named Facebook.

Nine months later, he moved on to launch the budget software Mint.com, but eventually realized he needed to pursue his own passions instead of building businesses for others. Last year, his company AppSumo generated eighty million dollars in revenue. Along his journey, he learned many lessons and took on some fun challenges to help others who want to scratch their entrepreneurial itch.

In Noah's book *Million Dollar Weekend*, he tells a story from 2013 when he took on a challenge to earn one thousand dollars of profit in just twenty-four hours from a brand-new business. In his course titled "Monthly1K," he teaches people how to start a side-hustle to earn one thousand dollars per month, while working only on their evenings and weekends.

He explained in his book, "My students were worrying because none of them had actually made their first one thousand dollars yet. They would get excited to start, but chicken out when it came time to actually sell their product." To show it didn't have to be scary, he took on a challenge.[1]

He told them, "I'll come up with an idea and make $1,000 in profit this week."[2] Part of the challenge was he couldn't use his current companies or networks; it had to be a fresh start.

He let the group of students come up with ideas for the business. Of the three options presented, he decided to scratch his own itch and sell something he personally loved—beef jerky!

After two minutes to decide on a name and ten minutes to build a one-page website, he did something most new entrepreneurs wait too long to do: he started acquiring customers. He sent off emails to his friends and family, then direct messages to connections through social media. When people bought, he asked them for referrals of their friends who might be interested. Just nine hours later, he crested three thousand dollars in sales, which resulted in over one thousand dollars in profit. Having the timeline of twenty-four hours drove him to focus on the activities that made the biggest difference.

But wait—don't you need a business license? And shouldn't you make sure you're protected with a structure like an LLC?

Yes, eventually. But that's not where you need to start. If you don't have any customers, you don't have a business. Noah didn't even have any jerky on hand and sold over three thousand dollars in product. Then, after knowing people wanted what he was selling, he got the product and began delivering.

Yes, he took orders before producing the product. As long as you set clear expectations and let your customers know a time frame they can expect fulfillment, it works. Noah explained many benefits come with starting this way: "You find out if you can actually get customers for your idea, you get money up front" to fund your procurement, and "You light a fire under your butt to get moving."[3]

It's easy to put off the tasks that seem overwhelming if nobody else is waiting on you. But by taking orders first, you're holding cash from your customers and cannot back out. Making just a handful of sales can be your point-of-no-return moment that drives your actions and keeps you moving forward.

Because Noah runs an eighty-million-dollar business, brushing off his quick win as something *you* couldn't do is easy. Surely there is more to it. In his book *Million Dollar Weekend*, he breaks down every step for you to play along yourself. The promise of the book is that in forty-eight hours, just one weekend, you can start a business that can make over one million dollars.

One of his tips to help you start is to not take it so seriously at first. If you decide to "launch a business," that can be scary. Instead, he encourages you to think of it as "trying an experiment" to get started. It takes the pressure off because experiments are meant to fail. In *Million Dollar Weekend*, Noah urges readers to "focus above all else on being a starter, an experimenter, a learner."[4] You'll use all your lessons as you develop and grow into your goal.

Noah goes on to teach us how to "stop thinking so much and go get busy," which means "starting small, starting fast, and not worrying about what (you don't) know."[5]

Noah had a massive impact on me, so I tried the "sell before building" method with amazing results. Not for a whole new business this time, but as a marketing "experiment" that was launched in less than twenty minutes.

At a business development event, Meaghan Likes was sitting next to me. A business owner and speaker, she was the first person I met during my inaugural trip to the same mastermind group two years prior. Leaning over during an event, she wrote "pre-holiday challenge" on the corner of my notepad. At the next break, she told me about one of her bookkeeping clients who recently had success getting new yoga clients with a twenty-one-day challenge. With the holidays coming up, starting on November 1 would be perfect timing to finish before Thanksgiving. I could give people a chance to get some results before launching into the holidays of food, drink, and desserts.

It sounded like a great idea, except for one problem. It was October 25. I told Meghan she had a great idea, but we didn't have enough time to build, launch, and market it before the start date. She looked at me and exclaimed, "You have six days!" Her eyes were wide with excitement, convincing me six days was plenty of time to try it.

As soon as we wrapped up the meeting, I took out my laptop and started. I built a quick and dirty payment form that could double as a landing page website and priced the challenge at twenty-one dollars. Then, we built the format that would allow me to sell now and produce later: the challenge would be delivered through daily text messages. All I needed to start was clients. Then, every day I could text them that day's workout and nutrition tips. I would build it as we went.

I typed up the first marketing text message and scheduled it for the next morning.

On the flight home, I finished most of the legwork that would make my day-to-day easier. I wrote up and scheduled a series of marketing emails and text messages that would go out to our current list of leads and former community members. I encouraged people to get started. The marketing centered around how the best way to stave off holiday weight gain is to start forming healthy habits in November, before the holidays have a chance to derail progress.

I didn't start the program because if nobody signed up I wouldn't need to. That's one of the perks of starting immediately and figuring out the details as you go. You eliminate wasted time and resources if the concept doesn't prove out.

When my flight landed, I checked the registration page. I already had three sign-ups! Two new members and one previous member had paid the twenty-one dollars for the challenge. Hell yeah! Those were three people who wanted to make a change and were ready to start. If I would have made excuses for why I didn't have enough time, they would still be struggling, unhappy, and looking for help with their problem.

I wrote out the workout format: three days of workouts followed by an active rest day. Iterating on the workouts to increase volume over the twenty-one days, I also included nutrition and motivation tips. The next day, my business partner and I used a tripod and an iPhone to film a series of videos explaining the format and movements in the workouts.

Over the next six days, sign ups kept rolling in, and on November 1 the pre-holiday challenge went live with eighteen participants. I scheduled two or three days of workouts at a time that went out in daily texts along with the iPhone video explainers. The participants submitted before-and-after pictures, and people got incredible results. In the end, four of them joined the Excel Health and Fitness community. With a client lifetime value of $4,500 and the twenty-one-dollar fee, the pre-holiday challenge resulted in over eighteen thousand dollars in revenue.

There were lots of excuses *not* to start. I could have completed a lot of tasks before making any real progress, but it's likely I would have never launched. First, I needed to make the perfect workouts and schedule. Then, talk to a designer to make a pretty landing page. Don't forget about the video editor to film and perfect the videos.

The truth is those things matter a lot less than starting. It would have taken weeks to get those tasks completed, and by then it would have been too late. I would have scheduled the launch for another time down the road, maybe even convinced myself that next November would be the best time. Other priorities would have come up, and while waiting for the perfect website and videos I may have never actually launched the challenge. By waiting to launch, I would have let people down who needed help. They would have been left to struggle when I could have helped.

Eighteen people who were looking for a solution were able to make progress on their goals. Four of them signed up to continue fitness journeys that will change their lives, and the business got a shot of growth and revenue. It happened because Meaghan encouraged me to start *now*. She didn't accept my excuses to wait and try later. It happened because right there at the table she motivated me to win my next hour.

As I reflected on this experience months later, I realized I had followed the WIN protocol:

Words: I told Meaghan I would do it.

Invest: By sending that first marketing text, people signed up and I was invested. I had to follow through.

Note Success: Every time someone signed up, I sent them a personal note congratulating them, which got me fired up from seeing the results.

Maybe you don't want to quit your job, and you don't have a company to run a marketing experiment. It still works if you just want a side hustle—something you can do on the weekends to bring in a little extra money. Or maybe you're looking for a hobby that makes you money instead of costing you cash.

My wife Jessica is a nurse. Between working a few nights a week and being a mom to our two young children, she was in desperate need of a hobby. Maybe golf? Nah, she thought, too much time and too expensive. Knitting or crochet? Too boring.

On a rare girls night out with two friends, they were talking about how much fun they had going to estate sales and finding cool vintage cocktail glasses, barware, and dishes. They decided to buy bigger houses to show it all off. Due to the California housing prices, that wasn't practical. Begrudgingly, they realized the need for only so many old cocktail glasses, no matter how cool they were.

The conversation led to their favorite part of estate sales—spotting the unique barware through all the rubbish. They had a plan: they would go to estate sales, buy vintage barware and kitchenware, then sell it on Instagram at market value.

When Jessica got home, she told me her plans and started talking about next steps. Did they need to form an LLC? Get a business license? Make a website? We had so much to do, when all they wanted was to buy old stuff and resell it to friends, family, and whoever found them on social media.

They knew exactly what they wanted but were lost in the minutia that was holding them back from starting. Forming an LLC and filing for a business would incur some costs in both time and money. It began to look like a big wall to climb, all for something they just wanted to experiment with.

Maybe it wouldn't work and they were the only ones who wanted old glassware. There was a chance nobody would buy any of their precious old stuff and it would turn into a hassle.

I encouraged them to just try it. If they didn't sell anything, they would not have any revenue. If they didn't have revenue, they didn't have a business and wouldn't need a business license.

They came up with a fun name, Serve It Up Vintage, and made an Instagram page (@serveitupvintage). They did not buy any ads. They just posted about their new venture on their personal pages and asked people to follow the new account.

Armed with a twenty-dollar bill and enthusiasm, they hit the estate sale circuit. Combing through the homes and belongings of one deceased old lady after another, they found some stuff they like. Through the clip-on earrings and rusting utensils, they realized what they didn't know exactly what to look for.

Knowing what they liked was one thing, but when it came to 1950s glass manufacturers there was a lot to learn. What cuts, styles, and patterns were rare and desirable? So, they went to the expert—Google Lens. Snapping pics and letting the search behemoth educate them worked wonders. They began recognizing familiar patters and the structures of different glass companies, and their uneducated guessing soon turned to educated decisions. With their bag of newspaper-wrapped breakable antique glasses, they went home feeling equal parts victorious and anxious.

After sorting and cleaning it was time to take pictures to create posts for the first vintage release. Between the three of them, they had precisely zero experience taking alluring product pictures or writing sales copy. Their proven methods of trial, error, and Google proved victorious once more.

Posting their first five items marked two to five times their investment, they asked people to comment or direct message them to buy. Two hours later every item was sold and paid for. Four were local, so they bagged and delivered the goods. But one purchaser was in another state.

The trio of vintage glass slingers had the same amount of experience packing and shipping fragile glass as they did taking product pictures. This time they relied on connections to get the job done. Our neighbor has a candle business and ships glass containers all over the country, so Jessica asked for help protecting the porcelain. Thirty minutes later, she dropped off a package to the post office, and the order was on its way to Texas.

The journey was littered with things they didn't know. Their enthusiasm and willingness to keep moving forward and figure out the details turned a fun idea into a profitable hobby in a week. They went from Google searchers to vintage glass experts. From listing their first collection to earning over ten thousand dollars in two years.

Winning your next hour doesn't mean you have the plan all laid out. It means you know what you want to do, and you begin making progress now. As you take the first step and start identifying best practices, you form patterns and rhythms that lead to success.

Strength coach, author, and American record holder Dan John was a big influence of mine when I first started competing in weightlifting. He was determined to stay active and strong as he was aging. Instead of just having the intention, he set up his life to force him to follow through on his ideals. In his book *Never Let Go*, he explained his methods for staying strong and active.[6]

If he was registered for a competition, he was compelled to train leading up to the event. In January of every year, he looked at the scheduled local weightlifting meets throughout the entire upcoming twelve months. He would pick one on the schedule every few months and sign up for them at that moment. Filling out the registration form and paying the fee in January, he committed to an annual schedule of demarcation points where he would have to be in shape.

A collegiate strength coach, author, athlete, and business owner, Dan John knows what it's like to juggle a schedule. I reached out to Coach Dan John to see if he still sets up his year in that way.

As I finished the question, he boisterously replied, "Of course I do!" He went on to explain that by taking that time early in the year to set a schedule, it helps him to roll with the punches. Coach Dan John explained that when you "plan the plan-able, if anything goes off script you have the bandwidth to deal with it."

I pressed on to ask if he had any instance in life where he just started before knowing the details of the *how* he was going to accomplish the goal. He was champing at the bit to answer.

"Well, yeah. Let's see...play football, throw a discus, get a D1 scholarship, write a book. Almost everything in my life. My number one success goal is to show up, number two is don't quit, and number three is ask questions. You gotta *do*. There's always going to be problems. Show up and fix the fixable."

Reaching Out to People

When it came to *doing*, I was slipping. One of my first assignments for writing this book was to make a list of people who could contribute to the topic and would be helpful to interview. I started off with the people who came to mind immediately—friends, former coaches and teammates, and other business owners I was already connected with. Those names sparked ideas for other people.

Along the way, I had some people who I knew had great stories, but they were a little out of reach. People who I almost left off the list because I've never spoken to them before or are "too famous" or "too busy" to talk to me. But those weren't reasons not to try, they were excuses I made up for them. I even found myself leaving friends off who I hadn't talked to in years and who have since became much more popular.

The funny thing is, it's just a list. Nobody knows who's on it except me and the publisher's staff. I could've written "Brad Pitt," and it wouldn't matter. And who knows—maybe he'd be down to talk.

Recently, I've been going through the list to see who I didn't make it to, and I found myself hesitant to reach out to some people. I'm sure you'll have the same experience when you go to win your next hour and someone who can help pops up in your mind. This is exactly what I did to get a hold of people. The first step is to realize they might say "no." And that's okay. In fact, by *not* asking them, you're already saying "no" for them...which is jacked up. Give them the opportunity to turn you down. Don't take that from them.

One example is Mario Lanzarotti. I've never met him in person, but his TED Talk inspired some of this content. I found him on Instagram and slid in his DMs. Here's exactly what I wrote:

What's up Mario! Your Ted talk about self-doubt inspired me. There are a few lines from it I quoted in the book I'm writing called "Win Your Next Hour" (and gave you credit, obviously). Are you open to a ten-minute phone call? I'd love to feature you more with some original "primary source" content.

He got back to me within a day and said he was honored to be an inspiration and would love to talk.

That led to a thirty minute long zoom call where Mario covered information from his talk along with other thoughts and ideas that helped shape more of the content. I used that same template with relevant changes to get on the phone with people like Mario who I never had talked to, as well as old connections I've lost touch with like bestselling author James Clear and prolific business mogul Noah Kagan. It even worked for strength coach Dan John, whom I've been a fan of for over a decade.

Of course, reaching out cold takes some guts. After typing up that first message, I sat there staring at it before sending. I was afraid Mario wouldn't respond or would reject me. Then I realized I needed to win my next hour and sent the message. I sent out another three messages right away while I was feeling brave. A few people ghosted me. Another had an automatic reply saying, "This email inbox is not monitored." But in the end, I got very few rejections. The people who did reject me did so kindly.

When you think of someone who can help you toward the next step in your goal, reach out to them. If they say "no," who cares? If you don't ask, it's already a "no."

Win Your Next Hour

Go start something now. Send a text to a friend and let them know what your dream is. Ask them if they think you can do it. And if you want to start a business, reach out to someone you know who would benefit from it and ask them to buy it now. Think of it as an experiment. Take

Noah Kagan's advice—"every experiment has within it the potential of unforeseen rewards that can change your life. *But first, you've got to start.*"[7]

CHAPTER 10

FROM HERE TO THERE

How far can you take it? Your idea went from a dream to a goal, and from a goal to reality. You started the thing that's been bouncing around in your head for years. The frameworks presented previously are often shown in examples of people going from zero to one. Creating something—a new business, a healthier you—out of nothing.

But that's not where the framework ends. You may want to scale your results from one to five, and maybe even five to ten. Let's learn how to apply the frameworks to bigger goals from people who have scaled companies beyond seven figures.

I reached out to three people who exemplify the processes presented in this book to scale their businesses and lives in big ways. Here is how you take your new adventure to the next level.

Bedros Keuilian

Bedros Keuilian was six years old when his father saved up enough money to bribe their way out of communist

Armenia. They landed in America with one hundred and eighty-four dollars to support their family of five.

Learning English in first grade, Bedros struggled through school. As difficult as the classwork was, relationships with other students were even harder. The language barrier mixed with economic struggles and differences of childhood experiences proved a challenging trifecta. Overweight and culturally disconnected, he found himself the target for school bullies. Over the years, he could communicate better and became more comfortable in the American school system.

Bedros threw himself into fitness. It was something he could control and helped him build confidence. After seeing his life change through the confidence he built, he wanted to do the same for others.

His new love of fitness paired perfectly with his desire to help others and led him to become a personal trainer. His business developed from training clients one on one to small groups in bootcamp style classes. And that's what led him to launching the very first Fit Body Boot Camp gym.

He explained to me, "Every time I started something, there was this internal calling. Call it God, or the universe, or whatever that is, is what I believe that internal nagging is. You have to lean into imperfect action. I realized if I don't, I'll be anxious due to the low-level regret."

As the gym grew, it was obvious he could only help a limited number of people in one location. It was time to turn his successful gym into a franchise.

And that's when he hit the wall. Working early mornings and late nights took a toll on his family life and health. Running a fitness business, he found himself overweight, overstressed, and unhappy.

His challenges continued to build until it all came to a head in 2013. In his book *Man Up*, Bedros explained, "I knew my business was struggling and that I had lost control of my employees and the direction that Fit Body Boot Camp was headed, so I hired a consulting company to help us. They were supposed to help create systems for my new franchise business. We were paying them $22,000 a month for their help—money that we did not have available and went into debt to obtain."[1]

But without changing his own habits and hang-ups, he was flushing the money down the drain. The debt mounted along with the stress. One morning while bending over to tie his shoes he felt his chest tighten up. He recalled, thinking he was having a heart attack, Bedros was convinced he would die and leave his two young children fatherless. As he made his way outside for help, the fresh air hit him and he could breathe a little easier. It was a panic attack.

He knew something had to give. Something had to change. That something was him. His poor leadership skills were driving his business and life further away from success. That's when he adopted a mantra that helped him stop procrastinating and living a chaotic life and start taking action. He told himself it was time to "man up" and take responsibility for everything in his life.

And he needed to start immediately. It was time to level up his leadership, and he needed to make the change at that moment. It wouldn't happen overnight, but if he didn't start, he was going to be bankrupt within weeks. Bedros had to win his next hour.

He started with finding his weak spots by writing down exactly which areas of leadership he was lacking. Accountability, vision casting, and organization. Boom! With an honest list of weaknesses, he had just won his last hour. He took those lessons and ruthlessly worked on himself and his leadership skills.

He realized fear was controlling his decisions. This led to poor management of his time and energy, and ultimately poor leadership. Working with business coach Craig Ballantyne (who had experiences with anxiety attacks himself, discussed in chapter 5), he fixed his time management and habits.

Next, he looked at his team and became the leader they needed. He communicated clearly and made decisions faster and with conviction. He defined the teams goals and held everyone accountable. His commitment to change his life and business worked, and he's never gone back.

Ten years later, Bedros' portfolio of businesses brings in annual revenues of two hundred million dollars. Leaning into imperfect action is what got him from an idea to his first business and from one location to a franchise with over six hundred locations worldwide. When I asked him about going from level one to five, and five to ten, he had complete clarity.

"People and processes to get from one to five," he explained during our interview. "From five to nine, that's when you need leadership. Fit Body Boot Camp scaled when I brought in leaders. You're able to scale faster with a great leader in the right role. Most people are focused on control, and that's a big mistake."

Bedros had learned how to lead and knew where the company needed to go. The vision was clear to him, but organizational structure and detailed accounting practices necessary for next level growth were not his strengths. After making a list of strengths and weaknesses, Bedros decided to "double down on [his] superpowers, and then find the people whose strengths compliment [his] weaknesses." Hiring an executive assistant who thrives on minute details and scheduling was the first step. That freed up his time to focus on the things that drove business forward.

And it all started with taking immediate action. It all starts with winning your next hour and being honest with yourself about your soft spots. Then attack those weaknesses vigorously.

Mark Bell

In 2010, after tearing his pec muscle, world record holding powerlifter Mark Bell was looking for a way he could continue to get stronger and still train his chest. A self-proclaimed "meathead" with the nickname "Smelly" seems like an unlikely character to grow a business. But he was endlessly curious, and that curiosity led him to developing an industry-changing product—the sling shot.

The sling shot is a piece of hardy, but stretchy, fabric that has loops on each end. By placing your arms through the loops, the wide fabric sits across your chest. That gives just the right amount of assistance in the most vulnerable ranges of motion, allowing you to perform pushups and bench press with correct form. Mark went on to get a US patent on the slingshot and has sold hundreds of thousands of them worldwide.

The success led him to develop more products and grow his business into the millions. Mark's accomplishments now range from squatting over one thousand pounds to becoming an inventor and entrepreneur. He and his wife, Andee, own and operate a series of businesses including supplements and a widely successful podcast. He continues to grow and reinvent himself. Just last year, the once three-hundred-and-sixty-pound Bell ran the Boston Marathon. I reached out to Mark to talk to him about his continued and growing success.

He described how he loves to start, and then see where things go.

Mark explained during our call that he likes "to play around for a little while before setting a huge goal. Like a little kid—I'm going to bounce a ball against a wall and see how it comes back." He then takes that feedback and uses it for further development. Listening to customers and the market have been critical to his success.

He continued, "You get a ton of feedback. People will tell you what they like or don't like, either with their words or their dollars."

For example, a few years ago he started a supplement company, Within You. The first products were selling pretty well, but when they released the Steak Shake, a protein powder that includes various animal organ meats such as kidney and liver powder, the company took off. Leaning into that success, they now buildout more products in line with what their customers have voted for with their reviews and dollars.

He also established a pattern of success before building further in his new athletic adventures. Before he began running, he went on walks every day for years as a form of exercise. One day, the sun was out and he was feeling good. On a whim, he decided to run to the next corner. It felt pretty good, so a few minutes later he ran another hundred yards. The next day he ran a little more. Eventually, he started off his routes running, and one day when he realized he was halfway through the route, he finished it and ran the entire way. Within a year of that first run, he completed a marathon.

Mark encourages people to do stuff that builds a belief in yourself, to rely on your strengths in different areas, even when it's hard.

He went on to explain, "Due to the shape you're in, where you are in life, your experiences shape decisions. Maybe your background is full of hard times; you remember every negative thing people said about you, or you had shitty parents." To overcome these obstacles, he encourages you to look at your experiences and use the success you've already had as a jump off point. "Everyone has a little skill set in something. You build confidence and learn to transfer it over to other areas. Either build confidence in something else or build a small amount of confidence in that thing you're starting."

Noah Kagan

In chapter 9, we talked about Noah Kagan and his experience going from number thirty employee at Facebook to serial entrepreneur. He has more experience helping people get from zero to one than anyone I know. He's sold thousands of his course called "Monthly1K" that teaches people how to start a side hustle that will make them and extra one thousand dollars in profit a month.

I asked him, "What holds people back from starting?" His initial glib response quickly turned insightful.

"Starting—" He chuckled, before continuing. "What holds them back is a number of reasons, but it's the feeling of not being ready. They're taught in school to go learn a bunch and be more prepared. If you go deeper than that, they're afraid. Afraid of rejection, afraid of 'what happens if someone doesn't like me.' Then deeper than that, they're saying 'am I a good person, am I worthy, can I be loved?'"

Noah went on to recall a story about someone he met the day before. An extremely intelligent computer programmer who was working on an app for other programmers. He's read a lot of business books and has spent six months building the app without a single customer. He wanted to keep building the app, but after reading Noah's book *Million Dollar Weekend*, he contacted one potential customer and made five hundred dollars that weekend.

He continued to explain. "The biggest thing holding them back is themselves and realizing that things can actually be started a lot quicker than they realize."

Noah has always been a good starter. And hopefully, if you've made it this far, you've started your journey as well. Early in our conversation, Noah commented that he hopes people don't finish his book, and don't finish mine. "I hope your book, Danny, gets them to stop reading and get started."

I agree. I'd love for you to finish the book, but more than that I'd love for you to have started your project and read this while on your journey. We both want you to start now.

Noah explained, "I think people put too much pressure that they have to succeed and it's all or nothing. One of the best mindsets around that is, can you start small? Start right now. Start small. And how can we not put so much pressure? It's just practice! When you start thinking about it as practice versus a profession or versus the final thing, it really puts in perspective the less significant it is, and you actually have more fun with it! It's just practice."

Getting small wins consistently add up. After initially starting, continuing is a series of winning your next hour over and over again. One reason I reached out was to find what got him from employee to the founder of an eighty-million-dollar business. Not just going from zero to one, but from one to *N*.

He explained to me when he was younger he "started too many things and didn't stick with them long enough." What made the difference was realizing his strengths and leaning into them. He found success by "embracing my zero to one, and then finding people around me who are very good at one to N. And then developing my one to N."

This idea of finding people who compliment your weaknesses is similar to what got Bedros from broke to two hundred million dollars in annual revenue. It's a theme that has come up time and time again throughout my conversations and research. It's okay that you can't do it all yourself. It's actually better; success is much more fun when it's shared with others.

Win Your Next Hour

After you've started, you'll run into situations where you feel stuck. The way out? The same way you started the first time. Use the Win Your Next Hour frameworks to start on a solution: Tell a trusted friend or advisor of the problem. Invest your time, energy, or money in a solution. Track results and learn what worked and what didn't. Most of all, win your next hour by taking action.

THE SECRET WEAPON

You've made it...this far.

Throughout the book, we have looked at many different skills, techniques, and frameworks to help you get started and keep going. One thing holds them all together: people.

In the first three chapters, you learned the WIN concept—words, invest, and note progress. *Words* goes first, is arguably most important, and revolves around people. You have to use your words and make a statement to those who you trust and will hold you accountable.

But you can rely on others for much more than sounding boards to throw ideas off. People will be a huge part of your motivation to stay on track and act courageously when scared.

When lacking courage, focusing on how your goal will help other people will be the extra push to step out of your comfort zone. If you're only thinking about how you will benefit, it's easy to procrastinate. After all, you're only letting yourself down. And thinking you're only hurting yourself isn't great motivation, especially if you're afraid of rejection or failure. Much more urgency and motivation are involved when you think about how you could be helping other people and how your procrastination is hurting them.

When discussing finding courage to move forward with Noah Kagan, he mentioned, "The thing about fear of rejection, the fear of not being worthy...ways to overcome it: help one person. Confidence is built through courage, and if you help a person you feel damn good about it. And that's how you can also get started right now. People don't realize they can get started right now."

Back to the example of starting a coffee trailer from earlier chapters. Where are you going to park it? You can take a table out to that spot tomorrow and serve people coffee! If they don't have any other option for amazing tasting coffee, you're doing them a service. You'll see how happy they are to have a great morning brew at a spot they couldn't get one before. Seeing their joy will encourage you to keep going.

If you want to get into photography, book a photoshoot with your brother's family. Then see how happy they are when you deliver the pictures that will help serve as memories for the rest of their lives.

Start helping someone with their food choices if you want to be a nutrition coach. Within weeks they'll be getting results, and their progress will be motivating for you both.

You'll find courage and fulfillment in helping other people, which is a sign you are going in the right direction. Focus on that feeling, and find what makes you happy. For many, it's actually the pursuit, the journey, the trying. Enjoy the challenges and struggles because whether you accomplish the big thing, so much of your life is the trying.

During our conversation, Noah also cautioned thinking about the end goal as the sole purpose of the pursuit.

He said, "I would definitely put a yellow flag on 'when I get there, I'll be happy.' Because let's say you get to this next hour and you win a customer, you win a physical thing, or you win parenting—you're still you." He went on to explain, "Just because you get these accomplishments isn't going to change how you feel about yourself."

Yes, you will gain confidence, which will embolden you to continue and take more risks and challenges. But if you don't like yourself, you won't *feel* much differently.

You should absolutely be chasing down your dreams and goals. But if the only person benefiting is yourself, you'll discover your new dream life is ultimately unfulfilling. Especially if you got there in ways you're not proud of.

Going forward from here, focus on two things:

1. How winning your next hour will benefit others?
2. What type of person do you need to be to accomplish your goals?

You'll ultimately find fulfillment by helping others and becoming someone you're proud of. And if you do fall short of the goal, you'll be fine. The lessons learned will help you with the next attempt. You won't be starting from zero; you'll be starting with valuable experience to grow from. The new and improved version of yourself will be ready for the next challenge. As a bonus, at least you helped someone.

Now it's up to you. What have you *done* with the information? If you haven't taken any action yet, put this book down right now and send a text message to someone. You don't even have to wait for your next hour. You can win *this hour.*

ACKNOWLEDGMENTS

Thank you to my wife, Jessica. Your belief in me and support of my projects are appreciated more than you know. I value your feedback more than anyone and appreciate everything you do for our family. Thank you to our daughters, Maddie and Norah. The lessons learned and relearned through being a father have made a tremendous impact.

Jeff, thank you for dragging me through Alaska and giving me the full experience. Our time together and your writing have been a massive inspiration in my life.

Thank you Coach Spitz and all my teammates at California Strength. I will always look back at the valuable lessons about life, comradery, coaching, and sport. I will always be a proud Cal Strength soldier.

Thank you Dean and Buddy, my business partners. You've both taught me so much about myself and how to work with others to create something truly special. Thank you Nick, who first gave me an opportunity at business ownership. You taught me what being unselfish looks like.

Jory, thank you for your generous time and effort creating videos that were a huge part of the early pre-launch success.

Finally, thank you everyone who was a part of the pre-launch. Although your financial backing was crucial, your belief in me and eagerness to support me has been overwhelming. I look at this list and am brought to different times in my life when each of you had an impact on my development has a leader, coach, father, and person. Thank you.

Bethany Acquistapace
Jesse Adams
James Aftosmis
Dawnia Alcodia
Ben Alderman
Caleb Allen
Ariana Altamirano
Jon Alton
Miguel Alvarez
Chris Amenta
Armen Amirian
Chris Andaya
Robert Anderson
Rob Anderson
Dolly Anderson
Chad Augustin
Tammy AultAlex Avila
Jenn Azevedo
Ann E Baker
Benjamin Barker
Jennifer Barker
Lynsey Barrow

Peter Bauman

Ryan Beall

Terri Beam

Joe Beck

Daniele Beeler

Chuck Bennington

Jamie Lynn Bianchi

Dimos Birakos

Tania Black

Nicole Blackwell

Daniel Borba

Vincent Bordi

Billy Boutwell

Justin Boyd

Richard Boyd

Travis Brading

Jessica Brakkee

Adrian Brandrup

Toni Bravo

Erika Brenner

Janna Brocchini

Mike Brown

Sonia Brown

Matthew Bruce

Jim Burau

Blaine Burgess

Oren Burks

Derrick Burnett

Briana Cady

David Calderon

Freddy Camacho

Ricky Campos

Suzi Cancar

Angel Cardenas|

Hector Carrasco

Karina Carrillo

Marko Carrion

Rachel Castillo

Adee Cazayoux

JC Chanowsky

Sophany Chhim

Abdiel Chiquito

Craig Cirillo

Patrick Clark

Jennifer Coenenberg

Shannon Cole

Courtni Coleman

Nina Coomes

Kevin Cornell

Kaleo Cornwell

Adam Cortez

Josh Cosio

John Crowe

Yancy Culp

Gino Da Rosa

Jeff Daley

Alfred Daos

Clay Davis

Seth Davis

Mark DeJong

Shu Dejong

Ravneet Dhillon

Brock Dias

Gina Dickman

Ralph Dominguez

Tim Donegan

Del Dukart

Michelle Duran

Sam Durham

Nicole Duso

Karl Eagleman

Danny Ear

Grace Einterz

Josh Emmett

Jared Enderton

Zach Even—Esh

Heather Everhart

Jennifer Faria

Lily Farmer

Nathan Farrier

Rob Fasani

Grace Fernandes

Jason Ferruggia

Marcus Filly

Ivan Flores

Josh Forrest

Paul Frantellizzi

Hayley Friedman

Aaron Fritz

Shaun Fulford

Felicia Galindo

Mark Gallo

Brian Ganz

Erin Garcia

Logan Gelbrich

Kornel George

Markus Gerszi

Zack Gibson

Jennifer Gil

Betsy Gish

Ajay Goel

Mitch Gomez

Julia Gongora

Marco Gonzales

Travis Gooch

Serena Goode

Mike Graber

Jordan Grabinoski

Sid Graef

Zeke Graf

Dillan Grant

Isaac Gross

Juan Guadarrama

Joey Guarascio

Kathleen Guion

Carlos Gutierrez

Dee Dee Hagen

Ryan Haggadone

Aaron Hanford

Levi Hanzel-Sello

Joseph Harai

Rebekah Hardick

Spencer Hardin

Chris Harp

Christian Harris

Kelsey Hecker

Aimee Hensley

Robby Hernandez

Marco Hernandez

Nicolas Herrera

Willie Herrer

Asaron Hinde

Erin Hines

Korey Hines

Chris Hintz

Bud Hitchcock

Jeremy Hobbs

Luka Hocevar

Katie Hogan

Toralyn Hohn

Sam Holmes

Lunaa Hong

Nicholas Hoyer

Jenni Hunt

Brian Hunt

Lisa Hydorn

Rick Inderbitzin

Jay Itagaki

Madison Jackson

Alexander James

Jeromy Jimenez

Richard Joaquin

Erica Johns

Katy Johnson

Jacquetta Jones

Tom Kallas

Jon Karmazyn

DJ Kastrup

Shondra Kaufman

Tonya Keener

Joseph Keith

Cayla Kent

Sargon Khizeran

Joseph King

Lacee King

Patrick King

Ashley and Joe Kirsch

Eric Koester

Jason Lacayo

Christine Lagorio

Drew Larison

Brad Layous

Leslie LeBaron

Jovani Lechadores

Alan Lee

Michael Lehr

Brian Lehr

Leah Leong

Kenneth Leverich

Brett Lewis

Andy Lewis

Meaghan Likes

Mitch Lopez

Hernan Lopez-Flores

Maria Lorenzana

Ben Lucchesi

Malcolm Luckie

Maggie Ludwig

Aaron Lutz

Jessica M Vaughan

Laurie Macias

Ashley Maharas

Jeremy Main

Andrew Maine

Chris Malone

Lindsey Marcelli

Kris Mares

Lynn Marleau

David Marques

Marcus Martinez

Daniel Martz

Trenton Mason

Charm Mathis

Jonathan Maynard

Jacob McCormick

Crystal McCullough

Chris McDermott

Alexander McGarry

Luisa McKee

Mack McKee

Robby Mclaughlin

Chuy Medina

Jonathan Meek

Natalie Mendoza

Steve Merchant

Tracy Meredith

Adam Merrill

Ryan Metzger

Steven Miller

Ellia Miller

Ian Miller

Lauren Miller

Chris Minten

Monica Molthen

Mikayla Montiel

Dale Moody

Ethan Moore

Blair Morrison

Peter Munoz

Jennifer Nichol

Kat Nieto

Mark Novak

Jorilyn Novotny

Aimee Ochoa

Noah Ohlsen

Marc Anthony Ortiz

Thomas Owens

Antonio Oyarzabal

Jason Pardue

Micah Payton

Kari Pearce

Becky Peck

Ken Peelman

Lori E. Pellegrino-Jackson

Amanda Perez

Tori Perez

Jackie Perez

Chris Perry

Ashley Peters

Gina Peverini

Sherry Peverini

Jarrett Pflieger

Wes Piatt

Dan Pilkington

Dan Platta

Sara Price

Travis Price

Jake Pudenz

Kurtis Rayfield

September Reeves

Jaysen Reindel

Lantz Rey

Rosie Reynolds

Rod Richard II

Michael Richards

Nate Richie

Sean Rigsby

Justin Riley

Paul Riva

Ronnie J Rodrigues

Jenna Rodriguez

Julian Rodriguez

Beejan Roohian

Kevin Rooney

Sean Rosander

Eric Roza

Chase Russell

Casey Ryan

Amy Saal

Jose Salas

Alfredo Salmeron

Kenny Santucci

Jordan Sares

Elliot Schnabel

Todd Schneberk

Cindy Schone

Caroline Schulte

Laurie Schwartz

Casandra Shamblin

Nick Shaw

Charles Shipman

Donovan Shiveley

Aaron Shockey

Sandeep Sidhu

Simran Sidhu

Joe Siler

Connor Silverstein

Rebecca Sims

Peter Sites

Jared Skinner

John Slater

Katera Snelling

David Spitz

Tom Sroka

Jason Starks

Katie Stolar

Andrew Stormer

Gabe Subry

Prakash Surya

Matt Tafoya

David Tao

Pete Taylor

Ryan Teicheira

Scott Thornton

Joann Tilton

Gabe Torres

Eric Tower

Bryan Townsend

Leah Truelove

Carol Urban

Chico Valadez

Kim Valentine

Sarah Vazquez

Tim Vick

Daniel Walter

Shannon Wanta

Sean Waxman

Ronnie Webb

Ginny Wertman

Michael Wesselink

Mariah Wheeler

Sumi Wideman

Erin Williams

Jeremy Williams

Chris Williams

Kristen Williams

Doc Williams

Dominique Williams

Stasia Wirth

Jenyfer Wood

Michael Wright

Eugene Yasutomi

Carly Young

Britny Zierenberg

APPENDIX

Win Your Next Hour

Chapter 1

1. Mario Lanzarotti, "Stop Doubting Yourself and Go After What You Really, Really Want | Mario Lanzarotti | TEDxWilmington," May 26, 2022, Wilmington, DE, TEDx Talk, 00:16:25, https://youtu.be/DmeOX5Zu36M?si=ozBRTUgbn—bMSKY.

2. Marielle Mohs, "Macklemore Tour stop in Minneapolis results in unforgettable moment for one superfan," *Local News* (blog), *CBS News*, October 9, 2023, https://www.cbsnews.com/minnesota/news/macklemore-tour-stop-in-minneapolis-results-in-unforgettable-moment-for-one-superfan/.

Chapter 2

1. Mario Lanzarotti, "Stop Doubting Yourself and Go After What You Really, Really Want | Mario Lanzarotti | TEDxWilmington," May 26, 2022, Wilmington, DE, TEDx Talk, 00:16:25, https://youtu.be/DmeOX5Zu36M?si=ozBRTUgbn—bMSKY.

2. Ibid.

3. Peter Bregman, 2012. "How to Start the Big Project You've Been Putting Off," *Career* (blog), *Psychology Today*, February 13, 2012, https://www.psychologytoday.com/us/blog/how-we-work/201202/how-to-start-the-big-project-youve-been-putting-off.

4. Stephen King, *On Writing: A Memoir of the Craft* (New York: Scribner, 2010), 269.

5. Benjamin Hardy, "The 100 Percent Rule That Will Change Your Life | Benjamin Hardy | TEDxKlagenfurt," August 1, 2019, Klagenfurt am Wörthersee Austria, TEDx Talk, 00:17:23, https://youtu.be/vj-91dMvQQo?si=QQvElmEAZYCeUZ6f.

6. Ibid.

7. Benjamin Hardy, "The 100 Percent Rule That Will Change Your Life | Benjamin Hardy | TEDxKlagenfurt," August 1, 2019, Klagenfurt am Wörthersee Austria, TEDx Talk, 00:17:23, https://youtu.be/vj-91dMvQQo?si=QQvElmEAZYCeUZ6f.

8. Ibid.

Chapter 3

1. Bronnie Ware, *The Top Five Regrets of the Dying: A Life Transformed By the Dearly Departing* (California: Hay House, 2019), V.

2. Angela Schroeder, *The Courageous Mind* (Washington, DC: New Degree Press, 2022), 28.

3. Emily Jaensen, "Six Behaviors to Increase Your Confidence | Emily Jaenson | TEDxReno," August 10, 2022, Reno, NV, TEDx Talk, 00:10:12, https://youtu.be/IitIl2C3Iy8?si=Yeo0eWEzEffN6NqU.

4. Ibid.

5. Emily Jaensen, "Six Behaviors to Increase Your Confidence | Emily Jaenson | TEDxReno," August 10, 2022, Reno, NV, TEDx Talk, 00:10:12, https://youtu.be/IitIl2C3Iy8?si=Yeo0eWEzEffN6NqU.

6. Rosabeth Kanter, *Confidence: How Winning Streaks and Losing Streaks Begin and End* (New York: Three Rivers Press, 2006), 32.

7. Emily Jaensen, "Six Behaviors to Increase Your Confidence | Emily Jaenson | TEDxReno," August 10, 2022, Reno, NV, TEDx Talk, 00:10:12, https://youtu.be/IitIl2C3Iy8?si=Yeo0eWEzEffN6NqU.

8. Andy Frisella, "Win the Day, with Andy Frisella—MFCEO 107," *REAL AF with Andy Frisella*, released November 15, 2016, 00:70:00, https://andyfrisella.com/blogs/mfceo-project-podcast/win-the-day.

9. Ibid.

Chapter 4

1. James Clear, *Atomic Habits: An Easy & Proven Way to Build New Habits & Break Bad Ones* (New York: Penguin Random House), 31.

2. Ibid, 201.

3. Charlie Jabaley, "Delusional Optimist (How To Start A Winning Streak) | Charlie "Rocket" Jabaley | TEDxRoxburyPark," June 1, 2023, Beverly Hills, CA, TEDx Talk, 00:17:06, https://youtu.be/7lNq3slbftc?si=5AbALo-pBt1jVeoo.

4. John Protzko, "Kids These Days! Increasing Delay of Gratification Ability over the past 50 Years in Children," *Intelligence* 80 (May–June 2020): Introduction, https://doi.org/10.1016/j.intell.2020.101451.

5. Mark Twain, "How Mark Twain Beat Procrastination," *Level SuperMind* (blog), 2024, accessed January 24, 2024, https://level.game/blogs/how-mark-twain-beat-procrastination-2.

Chapter 5

1. Craig Ballantyne, *Unstoppable* (Texas: Lioncrest Publishing, 2018), 11.

2. Ibid., 78.

3. Craig Ballantyne, *The Perfect Week Formula* (Texas: Scribe Media, 2019), 112.

4. Wei-Ching Wang, Chin-Hsung Kao, Tzung-Cheng Huan, and Chung-Chi Wu, "Free Time Management Contributes to Better Quality of Life: A Study of Undergraduate Students in Taiwan," *Journal of Happiness Studies* 12, no. 4 (July 2010): 561–73, https://doi.org/10.1007/s10902-010-9217-7.

5. John Powell, Happiness Is an Inside Job (Chicago, IL: Thomas More Association, 2017), 6.

6. Dan Sullivan, *The Gap and the Gain: The High Achievers' Guide to Happiness, Confidence, and Success* (New York: Hay House Business, 2021), 46.

Chapter 6

1. Gregg Glassman, "Fundamentals, Virtuosity, and Mastery," *The Journal* (blog), *CrossFit*, August 1, 2005, https://journal.crossfit.com/article/fundamentals-virtuosity-and-mastery-an-open-letter-to-crossfit-trainers.

2. Seb Ostrowicz, *The Glenn Pendlay Method, Glenn's Philosophy and Practice of Weightlifting Coaching* (New York: Powerful Ideas Press, 2020), 46.

3. Ibid., 52.

4. Seb Ostrowicz, *The Glenn Pendlay Method, Glenn's Philosophy and Practice of Weightlifting Coaching* (New York: Powerful Ideas Press, 2020), 52.

Chapter 7

1. Tim Sanders, "Put Your Network to Good Use," *Tim Sanders* (blog), June 9, 2009, https://timsanders.com/put-your-network-to-good-use/.

2. Jim Rohn, "You Are the Average of the 5 People You Spend the Most Time With," *Personal Excellence* (blog), 2024, accessed January 7, 2024, https://personalexcellence.co/blog/average-of-5-people/.

3. Darren Hardy, *The Compound Effect* (New York: Vanguard Press, 2011), 74.

4. Seb Ostrowicz, *The Glenn Pendlay Method, Glenn's Philosophy and Practice of Weightlifting Coaching* (New York: Powerful Ideas Press, 2020), 83.

5. Glenn Pendlay, "Dynamis," *Glenn Pendlay* (blog), July 1, 2018, https://glennpendlay.wordpress.com/2018/07/01/dynamis/.

6. Dan Wagner, "Alcoholics Anonymous: The 12 Steps of AA & Success Rates,"12 Step (blog), *American Addiction Centers*, May 10, 2024, https://americanaddictioncenters.org/rehab-guide/12-step/whats-the-success-rate-of-aa.

7. Practical Recovery, "In AA Social Support Is More Important than a Higher Power," 2024, accessed January 24, 2024, https://www.practicalrecovery.com/in-aa-social-support-is-more-important-than-a-higher-power/.

8. Craig Ballantyne, *Unstoppable* (Texas: Lioncrest Publishing, 2018), 115.

Chapter 8

1. Brianna Chu, "Physiology, Stress Reaction," *StatPearls* (blog), *National Library of Medicine*, May 7, 2024, https://www.ncbi.nlm.nih.gov/books/NBK541120/.

2. Aline Holzwarth, "The Power of Precommitment," *Resources* (blog), *Pattern Health*, October 10, 2018, https://pattern.health/power-of-precommitment/.

Chapter 9

1. Noah Kagan, *Million Dollar Weekend: The Surprisingly Simple Way to Launch a 7-Figure Business in 48 Hours* (New York: Portfolio, 2024), 65.

2. Ibid.

3. Noah Kagan, *Million Dollar Weekend: The Surprisingly Simple Way to Launch a 7-Figure Business in 48 Hours* (New York: Portfolio, 2024), 87.

4. Ibid, 10.

5. Noah Kagan, *Million Dollar Weekend: The Surprisingly Simple Way to Launch a 7-Figure Business in 48 Hours* (New York: Portfolio, 2024), 204.

6. Dan John, *Never Let Go: A Philosophy of Lifting, Living and Learning* (California: On Target Publications, 2019).

7. Noah Kagan, *Million Dollar Weekend: The Surprisingly Simple Way to Launch a 7-Figure Business in 48 Hours* (New York: Portfolio, 2024), 10.

Chapter 10

1. Bedros Keuilian, *Man Up: How to Cut the Bullsh!t and Kick @ss in Business (And in Life)* (Texas: BenBella Books, 2018), 42.

2. Ibid.

www.ingramcontent.com/pod-product-compliance
Lightning Source LLC
Chambersburg PA
CBHW070512160726
48003CB00004B/1533